Romantic Silk Ribbon Keepsakes

Romantic Silk
Ribbon Keepsakes

by
Mary Jo Hiney

Sterling Publishing Co., Inc. New York
A Sterling/Chapelle Book

For Chapelle, Ltd.

Owner: *Jo Packham*

Editor: *Malissa M. Boatwright*

Staff: *Marie Barber, Kass Burchett, Rebecca Christensen, Holly Fuller, Marilyn Goff, Michael Hannah, Amber Hansen, Shirley Heslop, Holly Hollingsworth, Susan Jorgensen, Susan Laws, Pauline Locke, Barbara Milburn, Linda Orton, Karmen Quinney, Leslie Ridenour, Cindy Rooks, and Cindy Stoeckl*

Photographer: *Kevin Dilley for Hazen Photography*

Photography Styling: *Susan Laws and Cindy Rooks*

If you have any questions or comments or would like information on specialty products featured in this book, please contact: Chapelle, Ltd. • P.O. Box 9252 • Ogden, UT 84409 • (801) 621-2777 • Fax (801) 621-2788

Library of Congress Cataloging-in-Publication Data

Hiney, Mary Jo
    Romantic silk ribbon keepsakes / by Mary Jo Hiney
        p.   cm.
    "A Sterling/Chapelle Book."
    Includes index
    ISBN 0-8069-8143-1
    1. Silk ribbon embroidery.   I. Title.
TT778.S64H563   1997
746.44--dc21   97-376
                                                 CIP

10 9 8 7 6 5 4 3 2 1

Published by Sterling Publishing Company, Inc.
387 Park Avenue South
New York, NY 10016
©1997 by Chapelle, Ltd.
Distributed in Canada by Sterling Publishing
c/o Canadian Manda Group
One Atlantic Avenue, Suite 105
Toronto, Ontario
Canada M6K 3E7
Distributed in Great Britain and Europe by Cassell PLC
Wellington House
125 Strand
London WC2R OBB, England
Distributed in Australia by Capricorn Link
(Australia) Pty Ltd.
P.O. Box 6651
Baulkham Hills, Business Centre
NSE 2153, Australia

Sterling ISBN 0-8069-8143-1

Acknowledgements

Some enter your life to open doors, some to present unimagined gifts, others simply to inspire and help you believe. To these women, I give thanks.

I never met Sadie, who became an entrepreneur half a century before the women's movement began. Dorothy, her daughter, carefully saved Sadie's belongings. One day in my young womanhood, Sadie and Dorothy's things became part of my life. The original Stationery Folder, reproduced on page 65, is one small example of the inspiration Sadie has been to me. I wish I could thank Dorothy for preserving Sadie's memory. In turn, I will also preserve her memory, and yours, Dorothy.

Mom taught me many things about sewing besides how to sew. Her love for and knowledge of fine textiles and excellent workmanship is the basis of my creative origins. My sister, Rose, is utterly unaware of the inspiration she has provided to me. That's one of the best gifts to give, isn't it?

Indroni and Marilyn believed in me when I was very low. More than that, they provided for me a real solution to difficult times. Their gracious manner is unmatched by anyone I know. Many times in my memory I replay their messages of utter delight at opening one of my shipments. This hurried world has forgotten the importance of kind and generous words.

But there was one day when time stood still, the day Jo called with my unimagined gift. Still and often she appears at my creative doorstep with hope in her arms.

There are many others, Lauren, Melanie, Saundra, Judi, Suzanne, Debi, Pam, Alexis, and Claire.

And then there was Mary Hackworth. I was a mere 21 years old when she entrusted me with her most valuable customers. Thanks Mary, wherever you are.

Contents

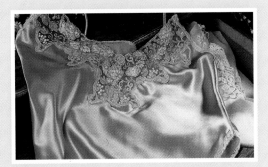

General Instructions

Projects in this book call for special embroidery stitches and ribbon work. Techniques are explained in General Instructions. Refer to these General Instructions to complete the project more easily and produce pieces that will last through the years.

Projects can be assembled by hand-stitching, machine-stitching, or glue of choice. Use the method that is most comfortable and convenient.

•Before Beginning

❖Gather materials and tools listed in materials and tools box with instructions for each project.

Assorted Ribbon

❖For ribbon embroidery a wide variety of ribbons can be used. Ribbons come in assorted patterns, colors, and sizes.

Brown Paper Bag

❖An opened brown paper bag is a perfect "drop cloth." Place cardboard parts onto paper bag while rolling with glue.

Cardboard

❖Heavy cardboard: Use crescent board, mat board, or process board. Heavy cardboard is thick and sturdy, yet thin enough to be cut with scissors. It can be found in hobby stores and art supply stores. The board should be white on both sides. Process board works best. If no other kind is available, ¹⁄₁₆" thick chip board can be substituted.

❖Lightweight cardboard: Use railroad board, poster board, or chip board. Thinness makes the cardboard pliable. Railroad and poster board can be white on both sides; chip board is gray. White board is preferred; gray board can discolor fabric.

Double-sided Fusible Web

❖This method is very easy. Follow manufacturer's instructions.

Embroidery Floss

❖Embroidery floss may be required. Colors are indicated in materials list. This 6-strand floss should be separated into one or more strands according to project instructions.

Fabrics

❖All designs can be stitched on specified fabric or fabric of choice. Choose any fabric in preferred shade. Embroider fabric by following Ribbon Embroidery Color and Stitch Guide.

❖Stretch fabric taut on a hoop or frame before beginning embroidery. Select one large enough to encompass entire design. If using a hoop, which may have to be moved across design, avoid snagging threads in worked area.

Glue

❖For any gluing steps where type is not specified use glue of choice. Never allow glue to show.

❖Craft glue: To laminate fabric to cardboard, use thin-bodied craft glue. It bonds fabric to cardboard without staining fabric. Consistency is perfect to paint onto cardboard using an old paint brush or paint roller. The laminating process is half the work and three times the bond when the right kind of craft glue is used. Craft glue can be used for box construction, but it needs to set up for each step and be held together with clothespins or masking tape until dry.

❖Hot glue gun and glue sticks: This is the preferred glue for box construction. Hot glue allows for an instant bond. Use the "cloudy" glue stick. Clear sticks do not penetrate fabric well for a good bond; yellow sticks are for surfaces like wood. Whenever hot glue is used, flatten thoroughly so bulk is eliminated.

❖Industrial-strength glue: This is a very strong glue and dries clear, but is extremely toxic. Use only in a well-ventilated area. Read manufacturer's instructions carefully. It can be used on difficult-to-glue materials like ceramic, rubber, fiberglass, plastic, wood, metal, concrete, and glass.

Hand-dyed Ribbon

❖The use of 4mm hand-dyed ribbons allow for terrific variation and color texture. These are available at quilt shops or can be dyed to desired color.

Knotting End of Silk Ribbon

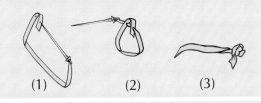

(1)   (2)   (3)

❖Drape ribbon in a circular manner to position end of ribbon perpendicular to the tip of needle. See (1).

❖Pierce end of ribbon with needle, sliding needle through ribbon as if to make a short basting stitch. See (2).

❖Pull needle and ribbon through stitch to form knot at end of ribbon. See (3).

Lace

❖Many lace patterns and lace color choices are available. Any lace pattern, old or new, large or small, can be embroidered over with ribbon by simply filling in the area of lace to be covered with ribbon stitches and French Knots. Lace and embroidery are accented with old pearls, bugle beads, and seed beads. Hand-stitching on lace, netting, and velvet adds a nice texture that cannot be achieved by gluing.

Manipulating Ribbon, Silk or Silk-like Ribbon

❖One of the most important aspects of silk ribbon embroidery is manipulation of the ribbon. For most stitches the ribbon must be kept flat, smooth, and loose. Use thumb and needle to manipulate ribbon while stitching or silk ribbon may curl and fold, affecting the appearance.

❖Follow the numerical order of stitches in Ribbon Embroidery Color and Stitch Guide for each project.

❖Untwist ribbon during each stitch and use needle to lift and straighten ribbon. Pull ribbon gently to allow stitches to lie softly on top of fabric. Exact stitch placement is not critical, but make certain any placement marks are covered by ribbon stitches. Extra petals or leaves can be added using leftover ribbon. There are no mistakes, only variations. Be creative with your stitching.

❖To end stitching, secure stitches in place for each flower or small area before beginning a new area. Do not drag ribbon from one area to another. Tie a knot on wrong side of needlework to secure stitch in place and end ribbon.

Marking Tools

❖Test marking tool of choice on fabric first to make certain marks are visible and can be removed easily. Always use a light hand when marking with any marking tool.

Needles

❖For ribbon embroidery, as a rule of thumb, the needle barrel must create a hole large enough for ribbon to pass through. If ribbon does not pull through fabric easily, a larger needle is needed. Also, needle eye must be large enough for ribbon to lay flat when threaded.

❖Beading needles are very thin, long needles with small narrow eyes.

❖Chenille needles are large and long-eyed with sharp points. An assortment package with sizes 18-22 is best.

❖Embroidery needles or crewel needles are fine, sharp needles with large eyes. Needle size will depend on ribbon or floss size. An assortment package with sizes 3-9 or 1-5 is best.

❖Milliner's needles are long, narrow needles with the same thickness top to bottom.

Old Paintbrush or Paint Roller

❖An old paintbrush or a 3"-wide paint roller spreads glue onto cardboard surfaces just like a paint roller spreads paint onto a wall. It is a wonderful way to achieve thorough coverage of cardboard surfaces. The roller can be washed out with soap and water and reused for many projects.

Rags

❖A wet rag and a dry rag are necessary to keep hands clean so fabric is not stained with glue.

Ruler

❖A ruler with precise measurements is essential. Yardsticks and cloth tape measures are not precise.

Scissors

❖Craft scissors: These are essential to cut cardboard shapes accurately. Designate a pair of high-quality scissors for cardboard cutting. They have a very refined cutting edge, which makes it possible to get into tight areas, and are very strong. If it is difficult cutting cardboard, thickness of the blades could be causing the problem.

❖Fabric scissors: Designate a special pair of scissors for cutting fabrics. Using fabric scissors to cut other materials will dull blades and make them less effective at cutting fabric.

Silk or Silk-like Ribbon

❖To complete each project, ribbon colors and quantities are outlined in materials list at beginning of each project.

❖Before beginning, press ribbon using low heat to remove creases. Cut ribbon into 18" lengths to reduce chance of ribbon fraying while stitching.

❖Because silk ribbon is delicate, it can easily become worn, losing some of its body. If this happens, lightly moisten silk ribbon and it will self-restore. Because silk is a natural fiber, there may be slight color hue differences between strands. Have no fear! The elegance of silk ribbon embroidery is accentuated by this subtle shading.

❖With care, silk-like ribbons such as satin, synthetic, or polyester ribbons can be substituted. Be aware, there are some differences in the way they handle. It is worth investigating.

Threading Ribbon on Needle

(1)   (2)

❖Thread ribbon through eye of needle. With tip of needle, pierce center of ribbon ¼" from end. See (1).

❖Pull remaining ribbon through eye of needle. See (2).

Tracing Paper

❖Tracing paper is a relatively transparent paper used to trace patterns and placement diagrams.

Transfer Paper

❖Transfer paper comes in many colors. Choose paper that is closest in color and tone to fabric but can still be seen. Be certain to follow manufacturer's instructions. To reduce number of marks on fabric, trace with dashed lines instead of solid lines.

Utility Knife

❖Use utility knife to score cardboard and to cut difficult shapes. Use caution and develop skill with this tool. Remember, a sharp blade is safer than a dull blade.

•Making Patterns and Cutting Fabrics

Materials

Tracing paper

Transfer paper

Manila folder or mylar

Tools

Marking tools: disappearing pen; dress-
   maker's pen; erasable pen; pencil

Photocopy machine

Scissors: craft; fabric

Straight pins

Tape: of choice

Transferring Pattern

❖If directions indicate to enlarge pattern, place pattern directly in photocopy machine. Enlarge percentage required.

❖Lay a sheet of tracing paper on top of full-size pattern and trace pattern onto tracing paper using marking tool of choice.

Pinning or Taping Pattern

❖Using straight pins, pin traced or photocopied pattern in place on fabric. Using tape of choice, tape traced or photocopied pattern in place on cardboard.

Tracing Pattern

❖Insert and pin or tape transfer paper between pattern and fabric and/or cardboard. Using marking tool of choice, trace around pattern. Transfer marks to fabric and/or cardboard.

❖If using light box method, tape photocopy of pattern or design onto window. Place fabric and/or cardboard over design. Trace around pattern. Transfer marks to fabric and/or cardboard.

❖For very precise patterns, tape photocopy or traced pattern onto manila folder or mylar. Cut out. Trace around pattern onto fabric and/or cardboard.

Cutting Fabric and/or Cardboard

❖Using fabric scissors, cut fabric according to project instructions.

❖Using craft scissors, cut cardboard according to project instructions.

Labeling

❖Always label each piece of fabric and/or card-board pattern immediately after cutting. Place fabric with corresponding cardboard piece.

•Assembling

Fabric-covering Tips

❖Use a fabric that will not stain when laminating fabric to cardboard. Most silks and lightweight polyesters will stain. Test by laminating onto card-board scrap.

Materials

For Laminating, Pad and Wrap, Scoring, and Wrap Method

Fabric: listed in project

Thread: listed in project

Needles: listed in project

Quilt batting: listed in project

Cardboard: listed in project

Tools

Brown paper bag

Glue: craft, thin-bodied; hot glue gun and
   glue sticks

Old paintbrush or 3" paint roller

Disposable plastic or tin dish

Precise ruler

Scissors: craft; fabric

Utility knife

Marking tool: of choice

Wet and dry rags

Laminating

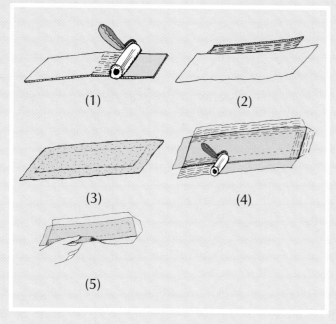

(1)

(2)

(3)

(4)

(5)

Wrap Method

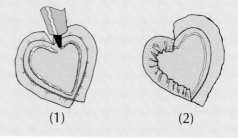

(1)

(2)

❖Place fabric onto work surface, wrong side up. Center cardboard over fabric. Trim out bulk from any corners. Using thin-bodied craft glue, apply glue around edges of cardboard. See (1).

❖Wrap edges of fabric over cardboard. Check corners for fraying fabric. Dab frays with glue if necessary. See (2).

Pad and Wrap

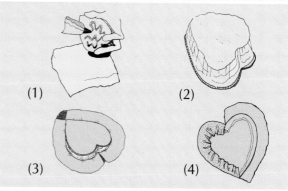

(1)

(2)

(3)

(4)

❖Prepare wet rag and dry rag for constant hand cleaning. Place or tape brown paper bag onto work surface. Pour enough craft glue into disposable plastic or tin dish to cover bottom of dish. Place cardboard onto brown paper bag. Place fabric wrong side up on work surface.

❖Roll glue onto paint roller in dish. Completely cover roller's surface, then roll off extra glue in dish. Paint entire surface of cardboard with glue. See (1).

❖Center glued side of cardboard on wrong side of fabric. Press in place. See (2).

❖Flip fabric and cardboard over and smooth fabric completely. Eliminate any wrinkles immediately. Pay special attention to edges. Fabric should adhere to cardboard everywhere, especially at edges. See (3).

❖Turn laminated cardboard over again. Trim out bulk from each corner. Use roller to paint edges of cardboard and fabric with glue. See (4).

❖Wrap edges of fabric over cardboard. Check corners for fraying fabric. Dab frays with glue if necessary. See (5).

❖Lightly glue surface of cardboard shape. Place onto batting. See (1).

❖Trim batting flush to cardboard's edge, beveling inward slightly. See (2).

❖Place fabric wrong side up on work surface. Center padded cardboard on fabric. See (3).

❖Apply glue 1" around one edge of cardboard and wrap fabric onto glue. See (4). On opposite edge, apply glue and wrap fabric onto cardboard as before. Pull fabric snugly. Trim out bulk from corners.

❖Continue to glue and wrap fabric onto cardboard a small amount at a time. Pull fabric snugly. Make certain glue is thoroughly flattened to eliminate bulk. Shape of cardboard should not be altered when fabric is wrapped.

Rolling Cardboard

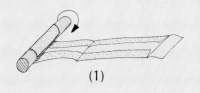

(1)

❖Using a round hot glue stick, or anything similar in diameter, roll box pieces as indicated in project into a circular shape.

❖Place cardboard on work surface. Place round hot glue stick at outer edge of cardboard. Wrap cardboard around glue stick without squaring off cardboard. See (1).

Scoring

❖Some projects with cardboard have score lines. Cover cardboard with fabric before scoring.

❖Place ruler onto score marks. Make certain to fold scores. Flip cardboard over and slice halfway through cardboard with utility knife at score marks, across width of cardboard. Do this by folding cardboard at score line and rolling over fold.

Lining Strips

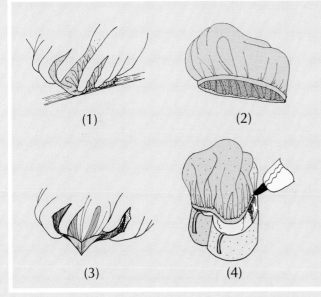

(1)   (2)

(3)   (4)

❖Finger-gather the lining fabric, right side up, onto strip while gluing in place. (An alternative is to gather-stitch around outer edge of lining fabric, ⅛"

from edge.) Adjust gathers to fit lining strip. Glue in place. See (1).

❖When all fabric has been glued to strip, strip becomes circular and inside out. See (2).

❖Flip lining strip fabric right side out. Turn down cardboard strip so that lining has finished edge. See (3).

❖Glue wrong side of strip to inside of box sides at top edge, thoroughly flattening glue. See (4). Begin gluing at center of strip. Where cardboard edges meet, adjust lining strip larger or smaller as needed, depending on fabric weight.

Basic Instructions to Collage Old Linens and Lace

Materials

Fabric: listed in project

Thread: coordinating

Lace: listed in project

Linens: listed in project

Doilies: listed in project

Tools

Iron and ironing board

Needles: listed in project

Sewing machine

❖Press each piece of linen and lace to prepare it for collage.

❖Remember two important factors when working on base fabric. Doilies are seldom used in their entirety, portions are used as bridges from one piece of lace to another. When used whole, a doily usually appears to be plopped in place, causing the eye to be drawn directly to it rather than seeing entire collage. The curved edge of doily is also easier on the eye than a straight edge and helps laces appear as if they belong together.

❖To collage laces, overlap ¼". Any greater overlap will cause individual lace textures to become muddled and lose their unique quality.

❖When ready to sew, use narrow machine-zigzag to stitch laces together rather than a straight stitch. The zigzag stitches get lost within the linens or laces.

❖Be prepared to move laces several times.

Painting Doilies

Materials

Doilies: listed in project

Acrylic paint: listed in project

Tools

Disposable paint dish or small aluminum pie pan

Cotton swabs

Textile medium

Soap and water

❖Textile medium is recommended to thin paint. It prevents acrylic paint from bleeding onto doilies and/or fabric.

❖Pour small amount of required acrylic paint into disposable paint dish or small aluminum pie pan. Thin acrylic paint with textile medium, following manufacturer's instructions.

❖Place required doilies on work surface, right sides up. Use cotton swabs to lightly paint center of doilies. Let paint dry thoroughly.

❖Clean up tools with soap and water

•Embroidery Stitches

Additional Stitch Information

❖This symbol (❂), when found in Ribbon Embroidery Color and Stitch Guide, indicates additional information that should be combined with directions for listed stitch found in General Instructions Embroidery Stitches.

Beading Stitch

Using doubled thread, come up through fabric. Slide bead on needle and push needle back down through fabric. Knot off each bead.

Bullion Stitch

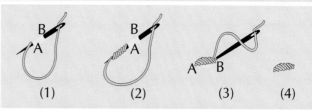

❖Bring needle up at A and down at B. Needle then must come back up at A, where it originated. Do not pull needle through. See (1).

❖Wind floss around needle number of times indicated in project instructions. Hold coil and needle firmly with thumb and forefinger and pull needle and ribbon through coil. See (2).

❖Turn coil back and insert needle back into fabric at B. To make bullion curve more, wind more floss. See (3).

❖Completed Bullion Stitch. See (4).

Cascade Stitch

❖Stitch or glue bow knot to fabric. Thread ribbon streamer on needle. Allow ribbon to twist. Go down at A. See (1).

❖Come up at B and go down at C making a small backstitch to hold cascade in place. Come up at D. Repeat for desired length for Cascade Stitch. See (2).

Colonial Knot

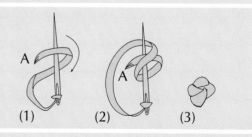

❖Bring needle up through fabric at A. Drape ribbon in a backward "C". Place needle through "C". See (1).

❖Wrap ribbon over needle and under tip of the needle forming a figure-8. See (2). Hold knot firmly on needle. Insert needle through fabric close to A. Hold ribbon securely until knot is formed on top of fabric.

❖Completed Colonial Knot. See (3).

Couching Stitch

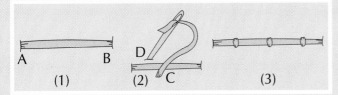

(1)   (2)   (3)

❖Complete a Straight Stitch base by coming up at A and going down at B (desired length of straight stitch). Make certain ribbon is flat and loose. See (1).

❖Make a short, tight Straight Stitch across ribbon base to "couch" Straight Stitch. Come up at C on one side of ribbon. Go down at D on opposite side of ribbon. This will cause ribbon to gather and pucker. See (2). The Straight Stitch base is tacked at varying intervals.

❖Completed Couching Stitch. See (3).

Feather Stitch

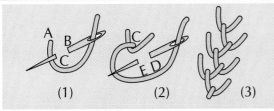

(1)   (2)   (3)

❖Come up at A, go down at B. Come back up at C, keeping the floss under the needle to hold it in a "V" shape. Pull flat. See (1).

❖For second stitch, go down at D and back up at E. See (2).

❖Completed Feather Stitch. See (3).

Fluting

Glue

❖Fluting is usually used as a trim. Glue one ribbon end to fabric or underside of cardboard. Loop ¼" deep and glue keeping ribbon angled. Repeat, making a series of even, angled loops.

Fly Stitch

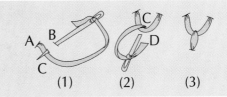

(1)   (2)   (3)

❖Bring needle up at A. Keep ribbon flat, untwisted and full. Put needle down through fabric at B and up through at C, keeping ribbon under needle forming a "U". See (1).

❖Pull ribbon through, leaving ribbon drape loose and full. To hold ribbon in place, go down on other side of ribbon at D, forming a Straight Stitch over loop. See (2). The length of Straight Stitch may vary according to desired effect.

❖Completed Fly Stitch. See (3).

French Knot

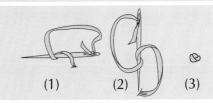

(1)   (2)   (3)

❖Bring needle up through fabric; smoothly wrap ribbon once around needle. (Ribbon can be wrapped one to six times around needle, depending on instructions.) See (1).

❖Hold ribbon securely off to one side and push needle down through fabric next to starting point. See (2).

❖Completed French Knot. See (3).

Lazy Daisy

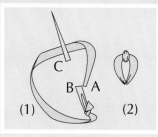

(1)   (2)

❖Bring needle up at A. Keep ribbon flat, untwisted and full. Put needle down through fabric at B and up through at C, keeping ribbon under needle to form a loop. See (1). Pull ribbon through, leaving loop loose and full. To hold loop in place, go down on other side of ribbon near C, forming a Straight Stitch over loop.

❖Completed Lazy Daisy. See (2).

Lazy Daisy, Bullion

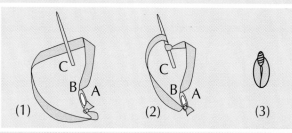

(1)   (2)   (3)

❖Bring needle up at A. Keep ribbon flat, untwisted and full. Put needle down through fabric at B and up through at C, but do not pull through. See (1).

❖Snugly wrap ribbon around needle tip one to three times, as indicated in stitch guide. Holding finger over wrapped ribbon, pull needle through ribbon and down through fabric. See (2).

❖Completed Bullion Lazy Daisy. See (3).

Lazy Daisy, Cross-over

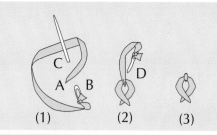

(1)   (2)   (3)

❖Bring needle up at A. Cross over to right of ribbon, and insert needle at B. Come back up at C and pull ribbon to desired shape. See (1).

❖Go down at D making a Straight Stitch to tack loop. See (2).

❖Completed Cross-over Lazy Daisy. See (3).

Lazy Daisy, Cross-over With Elongated Tip

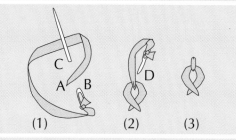

(1)   (2)   (3)

❖Bring needle up at A. Cross over to right of ribbon, and insert needle at B. Come back up at C and pull ribbon to desired shape. See (1).

❖Go down at D making a longer Straight Stitch to tack the loop. See (2).

❖Completed Cross-over Lazy Daisy with Elongated Tip. See (3).

Lazy Daisy, Knotted

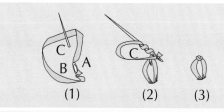

(1)   (2)   (3)

❖Complete as a Lazy Daisy. See (1).

❖Loosely wrap thread around needle tip one to three times. Holding finger over wrapped thread, insert needle down through fabric on other side of ribbon near C. See (2).

❖Completed Knotted Lazy Daisy. See (3).

Loop Petal Stitch, Loop Petal Stitch Variation

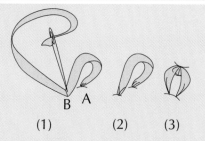

(1)   (2)   (3)

❖Bring needle up at A. Form small loop and go down at B, piercing ribbon. See (1).

❖Completed Loop Petal Stitch. See (2).

❖Use matching color of floss (1 strand) tack down center of stitches. Completed Loop Petal Stitch, Variation. See (3).

Padded Satin Stitch

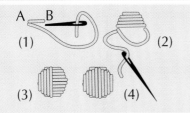

❖Using floss, bring needle up at A. Go down at B, and come up again near A to make loose, parallel stitches to fill pattern. See (1). Keep floss flat, stitching closely and evenly beside adjacent stitches. See (2).

❖Stitch again vertically for full padded pattern. See (3).

❖Completed Padded Satin Stitch. See (4).

Pistil Stitch

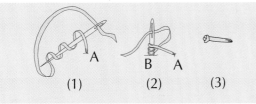

❖This stitch looks like a Straight Stitch with a French Knot on the end. Bring needle up through fabric at A. Smoothly wrap ribbon once (twice for a larger knot on end) around needle. See (1).

❖Hold ribbon securely off to one side and push needle down through fabric at B, desired length of Straight Stitch. See (2).

❖Completed Pistil Stitch. See (3).

Ribbon Stitch

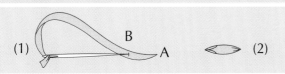

❖Come up through fabric at A. Lay ribbon flat on fabric. At end of the stitch, pierce ribbon with the needle. Slowly pull length of ribbon through to back, allowing ends of ribbon to curl. If ribbon is pulled too tight, the effect can be lost. Vary petals and leaves by adjusting length, tension of ribbon before piercing, position of piercing, and how loosely or tightly ribbon is pulled down through itself. See (1).

❖Completed Ribbon Stitch. See (2).

Ribbon Stitch, 1-Twist

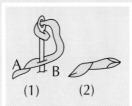

❖Bring ribbon up through fabric at A. Twist ribbon one time. Go down through ribbon at B. Slowly pull to back. See (1).

❖Completed 1-Twist Ribbon Stitch. See (2).

Ruffled Ribbon Stitch

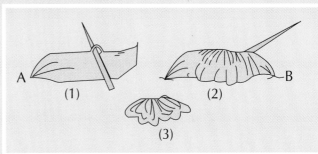

❖Knot one end of ribbon. Bring ribbon up a A. With needle, separate a strong thread from selvage of ribbon. See (1).

❖Pull thread to gather ribbon to desired length. Bring ribbon down through fabric at B. Secure ribbon to wrong side of stitching. See (2). Make a series of Ruffled Ribbon Stitches to appear as one.

❖Completed Ruffled Ribbon Stitch. See (3).

Running Stitch

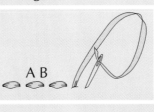

❖A line of Straight Stitches with an unstitched area after each stitch. Come up at A and go down at B.

Stem Stitch

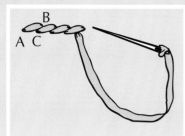

❖Bring needle up at A. Keep ribbon to left and below needle. Push needle down at B and back up at C.

Straight Stitch

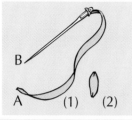

❖This stitch may be taut or loose depending on desired effect. Come up at A and go down at B. See (1).

❖Completed Straight Stitch. See (2).

Straight Stitch, 1-Twist or Twisted

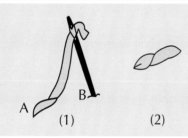

❖Follow instructions for Straight Stitch. Bring needle up at A. Twist before taking needle down through fabric at B. See (1).

❖Completed 1-Twist or Twisted Straight Stitch. See (2).

Tacked Loop Stitch

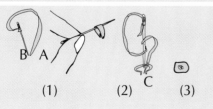

❖Bring ribbon to front at A. Insert needle into fabric at B. Allow loop to remain on fabric surface. See (1).

❖Come up at C piercing underside of loop. Wrap needle. See (2). Go down through ribbon and fabric, creating a French Knot.

❖Completed Tacked Loop Stitch. See (3).

Whipped Running Stitch

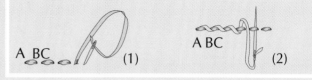

❖Complete Running Stitches first. See (1).

❖To whip Running Stitch, come up from under first Running Stitch at A; go over it and under second Running Stitch at B. (Be careful not to pierce fabric or catch Running Stitch.) Come up on other side of the stitch. Keeping ribbon flat, wrap ribbon over stitch and go under next Running Stitch at C. Continue in same manner. The effect can be varied by how loosely or tightly ribbon is pulled when whipping. See (2).

Wool Rose Stitch

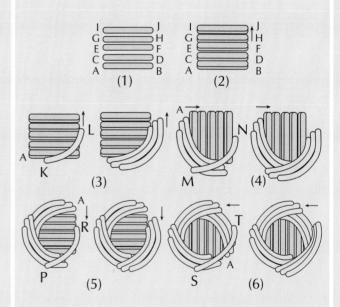

❖Bring needle up at A. Take needle back through at B and bring it to front one to two threads of fabric above A at C. Needle is slightly angled. Pull wool through so stitch lies flat. Make second stitch by going down at D. Work five stitches in all (A–J) to create a square. Carefully position needle in line for last stitch. Take needle through to back. See (1).

❖To complete second layer for a full padded square, bring needle up at C using same hole as previous row. Take needle back at D, using same hole. Do not pull too tightly. Wool should lie firmly over the first row. Work five stitches. See (2).

❖For first petal, bring needle up at K below padded square. Take needle down at L, approximately level with third row of padding. Petals are stitched over padded center. Come up beside K again and down at L for a total of three petals. See (3).

❖For second petal, rotate fabric clockwise. Bring needle up at M. Take needle down at N. Come up again at M and down at N for a total of three petals. See (4).

❖For third petal, rotate fabric again. Bring needle up at P. Take needle down at R for a total of three petals. See (5).

❖For fourth petal, rotate fabric once again. Bring needle up at S. Take needle down at T. Come up again at S and down at T for a total of three petals. Press firmly with thumb to "settle" the rose.

❖Completed Wool Rose. See (6).

•Using Ribbons
Additional Stitch Information
❖This symbol (❂), when found in Flower Work Color and Stitch Guide, indicates additional information that should be combined with directions for listed stitch found in General Instructions Using Ribbons.

Berry

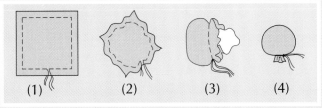

(1)   (2)   (3)   (4)

❖Gather-stitch all four edges of a square of ribbon ⅛" from edge. See (1).

❖Pull thread to gather slightly. See (2).

❖Place small amount of polyester stuffing in berry. See (3). Tightly gather and secure thread.

❖Completed Berry. See (4).

Circular Ruffle

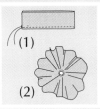

(1)

(2)

❖Fold required ribbon in half, matching cut ends. Gather-stitch along one selvage edge. See (1). Tightly gather and secure thread.

❖Completed Circular Ruffle. See (2).

Dahlia, Double Fold

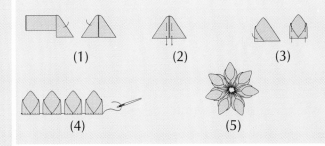

(1)   (2)   (3)

(4)   (5)

❖Fold ribbon. See (1).

❖Press folds with iron for crisp edge. Vertically pin folds to keep each petal pointed. See (2).

❖Turn folded ribbon over. Fold ends of ribbon inward to overlap ¼" at center. Pin ribbon folds. Repeat process for remaining ribbon lengths. See (3).

❖Chain gather-stitch all petals together ¼" above selvage edges. (This selvage edge is hidden within the ribbon folds.) Use doubled and knotted hand-sewing thread to gather-stitch. Backstitch at first stitch only to prevent the thread's knot from pulling through ribbon. See (4).

❖Once all petals are gather-stitched together, tightly gather and secure thread. Join last petal to first and secure thread again. Trim raw edges to ⅛" below stitches.

❖Completed Dahlia, Double Fold. See (5).

Dahlia, Single Fold

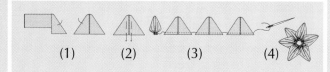

(1) (2) (3) (4)

❖Fold ribbon. See (1).

❖Press folds with iron for crisp edge. Pin folds in place. See (2).

❖Chain gather-stitch all petals together, stitching ¼" above raw edges. See (3). Tightly pull gather and secure thread. Join last petal to first. Trim raw edges ⅛" below stitches.

❖Completed Dahlia, Single Fold. See (3).

Daisy

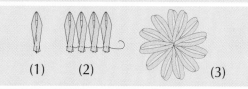

(1) (2) (3)

❖Fold each length of ribbon forward to overlap at cut ends. Pin to hold. See (1).

❖Chain gather-stitch all petals together. See (2). Tightly pull gather and secure thread. Adjust gather so petals are evenly spaced. Follow project instructions for joining last petal to first petal.

❖Completed Daisy. See (3).

Doily Rosette

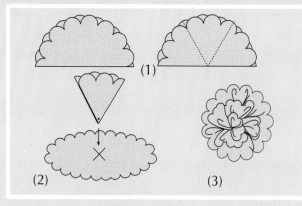

(1)

(2) (3)

❖Fold doily in half, then in thirds. See (1).

❖Fold bottom corner over. Glue bottom folded rolled edge to hold it in place. Place thin bead of

20

glue around center of second doily. Fold up around glue to slightly ruffle second doily. See (2). Glue first doily into center of second doily.

❖ Completed Doily Rosette. See (3).

Double-edge Gathered Rose

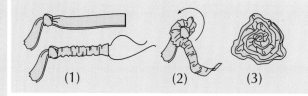

(1) (2) (3)

❖Using required wired ribbon length, tie knot at one ribbon end. Gently pull wires from opposite end on both edges. Move gathers down to meet knot while tightly gathering ribbon. See (1). Secure gathers by stitching at unknotted end and tying wires together. Trim wires to 5". Fold ribbon in half, matching gathered edges.

❖Beginning at knotted end, wrap folded ribbon around knot. Tack wraps in place. Continue wrapping folded ribbon in spiral fashion around center, building rose outward. See (2). Tack in place as needed. Trim wires.

❖Completed Double-edge Gathered Rose. See (3).

Finger Pleats

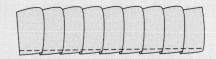

❖Pin ribbon pleats ½" deep and ½" apart, all in the same direction. Press. Stitch along one long edge of the ribbon.

Fuchsia

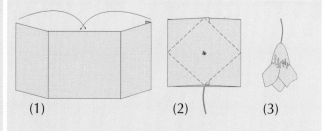

(1) (2) (3)

❖Fold one length of ribbon in half and crease center. Turn down one raw edge of ribbon ¼". Fold remaining raw edge of ribbon back so it overlaps center crease ¼". Fold turned-under edge of ribbon back to meet center crease. See (1). Pin to hold.

❖ Knot 6" length of floss or ribbon. Pull through "seam" from back to front side for fuchsia stem. Mark a diamond shape on fuchsia. Hand-gather stitch on diamond. Tightly gather stitch and secure thread. See (2).

❖Completed Fuchsia. See (3).

Garden Rose

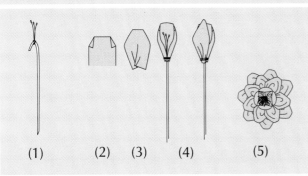

(1) (2) (3) (4) (5)

❖Fold down one end of lightweight wire with needlenose pliers to form loop. Slip purchased stamens up through wire loop and fasten to wire with thread. Looped end of the wire is top. See (1).

❖Cut ribbons to required length. Fold one length of ribbon in half, matching cut ends. At fold, fold one corner down ¼". Repeat with opposite corner. Glue folds in place. See (2).

Wrong side of petal has folds glued down. Repeat this step for all remaining petals, keeping like-sized petals together.

❖Stitch a deep pleat at cut end of petal so petal will cup. Repeat for all remaining petals, keeping like-sized petals together. See (3).

❖Stitch smallest petals onto wire. Take one of smallest petals and wrap it around top of stem, nearly covering stamens. Sew it to wire by wrapping thread around wire several times. Secure thread. See (4).

❖Wrap and stitch second petal onto wire directly facing the first one. Be careful to keep cut ends level.

❖Wrap and stitch third petal onto wire so it is at the side of first two. Place this petal a tiny bit lower than first two. Wrap and stitch fourth petal opposite third. Sew on remaining petals so they lie in-between first four. Be careful to keep cut ends level.

❖Completed Garden Rose. See (5).

Gathered Rosebud

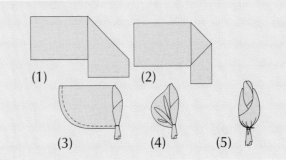

(1) (2)

(3) (4) (5)

❖Fold ribbon. See (1).

❖Fold again. See (2).

❖Roll folded end and secure at bottom of roll. Gather-stitch opposite end. See (3).

❖Tightly gather to form petal and secure thread. Wrap gathered petal around center roll to form bud. See (4).

❖Completed Gathered Rosebud. See (5).

Half Zinnia

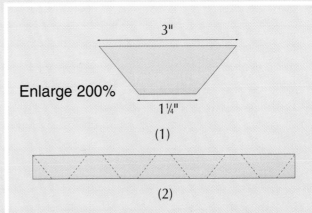

Enlarge 200%

3"

1¼"

(1)

(2)

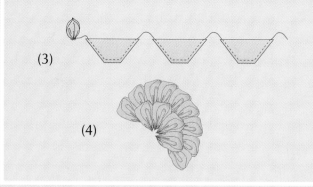

(3)

(4)

❖Cut ribbon into required number of petals, using pattern provided (enlarge 200%). See (1).

❖Alternate pattern onto ribbon when cutting petals to eliminate waste and utilize both ribbon shades. See (2).

❖Chain gather-stitch all petals together. Tightly gather stitches and secure thread. See (3).

❖Join last petal to first petal. Shape petals and pinch tips. Fold circular petal layer in half so that nine petals are on the bottom and four are on the top. Stitch to hold in place.

❖Completed Half Zinnia. See (4).

Knotted Mum

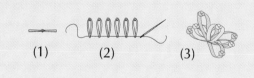

(1)   (2)   (3)

❖Tie a knot at center of each length. Place ribbons in like color piles. See (1).

❖Fold lengths in half with knot at top, matching cut ends. Alternate ribbon shades while chain gather-stitching them together, taking a ½" seam. See (2).

❖When all petals have been chained together, tightly gather and secure thread. Keep knotted ends facing same direction. Join last petal to first. Trim cut ends to ⅛" below stitching.

❖Completed Knotted Mum. See (3).

Leaf, Fabric

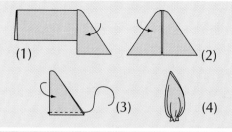

(1)   (2)   (3)   (4)

❖Press required strip of fabric in half, matching raw edges. Fold as shown. See (1).

❖Fold again. See (2).

❖Fold from center. Gather-stitch ¼" from raw edge. See (3). Tightly gather and secure thread. Trim raw edges to ⅛" below stitching.

❖Completed Fabric Leaf. See (4).

Leaf, Folded

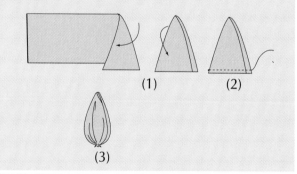

(1)   (2)

(3)

❖Fold ends forward diagonally. See (1).

❖Gather-stitch across bottom edge of folds. See (2). Tightly gather and secure thread.

❖Completed Folded Leaf. See (3).

Leaf, Gathered

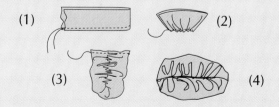

(1)   (2)

(3)   (4)

❖Cut ribbon to required length. Fold ribbon length in half, matching cut ends. Gather-stitch across bottom edges of ribbon. See (1).

❖Tightly pull gather stitch so that ribbon measures 1½" and secure thread. See (2).

❖Open ribbon and gather-stitch across top. See (3). Tightly gather and secure thread.

❖Completed Gathered Leaf. See (4).

Leaf Spray

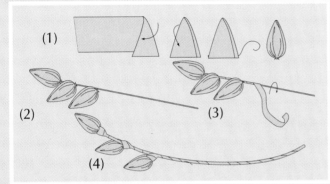

❖Cut ribbon to required length. Fold and stitch each into a Folded Leaf. See (1).

❖With a ½" loop in top of 6" wire, hot-glue three leaves onto wire, hiding loop in-between layers of top leaf. See (2).

❖Wrap with florist wire to hide raw edges. See (3).

❖Completed Leaf Spray. See (4).

Pansy

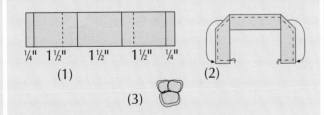

❖Mark each 5" ribbon length into ¼", 1½", 1½", 1½", ¼" intervals. See (1).

❖Fold edges together. Gather-stitch. See (2). Tightly gather and secure thread. Join last petal to first.

❖Completed Pansy. See (3).

Peach Blossom

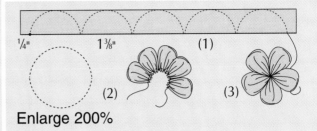

Enlarge 200%

❖Beginning ¼" from edge, trace five 1⅜" half circles on ribbon. Using circle pattern (enlarge 200%), butt circles up to each other. Trim fabric ¼" past last half circle. Gather-stitch on traced half circles with continuous gather stitch. See (1).

❖Tightly gather and secure thread. See (2). Join last petal to first and secure thread.

❖Completed Peach Blossom. See (3).

Pencil Violet

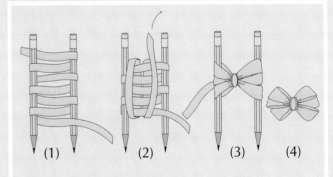

❖Cut ribbon into 12" length. Using two pencils held closely together, slip ribbon through center of pencils, with one ribbon end extended 3". Weave ribbon around pencils so each pencil has three loops of ribbon. See (1).

❖Take top end of ribbon and wrap it down, under, and up around the center of pencils two times while cinching the ribbon loops together. See (2).

❖Take opposite end of ribbon and wrap it up, under, and up around center of the pencils while cinching ribbon loops tighter. Take ribbon ends and tie them into a double knot at center of one side. Ribbon ends must be at opposite ends of wrapped ribbon before tying into knots. Slip violet off pencils.

❖Completed Pencil Violet. See (4).

Rosette

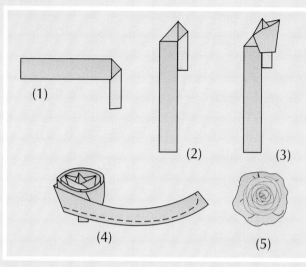

(1)

(2)

(3)

(4)

(5)

❖Fold length of ribbon down at right angle, creating a post to hold onto. See (1).

❖Fold folded end in half. Stitch in place securely with thread. See (2).

❖Continue rolling and folding ribbon. Stitch to secure. See (3).

❖When ribbon is folded and rolled half its length, hand-stitch a gathering stitch along the bottom edge of remaining length of ribbon. See (4). Tightly pull gathering stitch and wrap gathered section around folded rose. Stitch in place to secure.

❖Completed Rosette. See (5).

Single Petal Rose, Mountain Folds

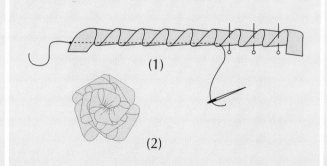

(1)

(2)

❖Single Petal Rose is a continuous series of mountain folds, similar in technique to Fluting.

❖Beginning with ribbon end facing downward, fold ribbon diagonally and forward and back so fold is ⅝" deep, or as deep as specified in instructions.

❖Fold ribbon diagonally forward and back, as for first fold. Pin bottom folded edge for better control.

❖After ten folds have been pinned, gather-stitch along bottom edge. Remove pins after stitching. See (1).

❖Fold, pin, and stitch another ten petals. If thread appears to be running short, pull up thread to gather ribbon.

❖Continue until entire length of ribbon has been stitched into mountain folds. Tightly gather and secure thread. Straighten folds so all are facing same direction.

❖Beginning at one end, roll folds into rose. Secure on underside as needed to keep rolls in place.

❖Completed Single Petal Rose. See (2).

Spider Web Rose

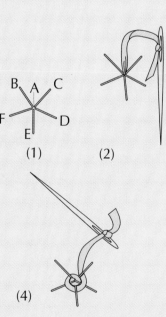

(1)　　(2)　　(3)

(4)　　　　　　(5)

❖Using two strands of floss or one strand of ribbon, securely work straight stitches to form five spokes. Work from center out, A to B, A to C, A to D, A to E, and A to F. These are anchor stitches to create rose with ribbon. See (1).

❖Bring ribbon up through center of spokes. See (2).

❖Weave ribbon over one spoke and under next spoke continuing around in one direction (clockwise or counter clockwise), until spokes are covered. When weaving, keep ribbon loose and allow it to twist. See (3) and (4). To end, stitch down through fabric along last row of petals.

❖Completed Spider Web Rose. See (5).

Turban

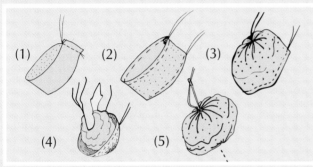

❖Fold ribbon in half lengthwise, matching cut ends. Stitch a ¼" seam. See (1). Turn right side out.

❖Gather-stitch around one long edge. Turn under remaining raw edge ⅛", while gather-stitching. See (2).

❖Pull gathers on one end as tight as possible and secure thread. Stuff Turban. See (3) and (4).

❖Pull gathers on remaining edge tight and secure thread. Take thread down through center of Turban to opposite side, then back up, and down again to tuft center. See (5).

Wisteria Spray

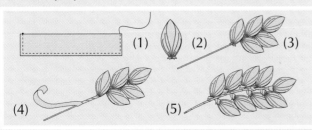

❖Cut ribbon into required lengths. Gather-stitch bottom and side edges. See (1).

❖Tightly gather and secure thread. See (2).

❖Stitch or glue gathered edge to looped end of length of wire. Repeat process for required number of petals on one wire, covering raw edges of previous petal with the next petal. See (3).

❖Wrap wire with florist tape for a finished look. See (4).

❖Completed Wisteria Spray. See (5).

Zigzag Ruched Flower

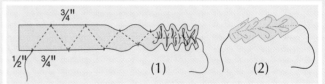

❖Starting ¼" from one end, mark ¾"-wide intervals for a total of thirteen intervals on one selvage edge and twelve on other edge. Gather-stitch, connecting dots in a zigzag fashion. See (1).

❖Pull gathers so ribbon measures 3". Secure thread.

❖Join last interval to first interval, aligning edges. Secure thread. Push ribbon ring so twelve petal edge is pointing inward. Join those twelve petals together at center of each petal.

❖Completed Zigzag Ruched Flower. See (2).

Zigzag Ruched Ribbon

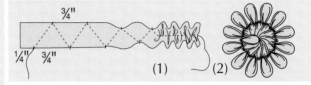

❖Starting ½" from one end, mark ¾"-wide intervals for a total of thirteen intervals on one selvage edge and twelve on other edge. Gather-stitch, connecting dots in a zigzag fashion. See (1). Pull gathers and secure thread.

❖Completed Zigzag Ruched Ribbon. See (2).

Bunny Tea Cozy

Materials

Fabrics: moiré, ivory, ½ yd.; moiré, peach, ⅛ yd.; organdy, 12" square; scraps, 3" x 3", green (6), ivory (6), peach (6)

Threads: coordinating

Silk ribbons: 4mm — aqua, lt. avocado, banana, lt. coral, dusty purple, dusty teal, forest green, glacier, gray purple, lavender, lichen green, maroon, mauve, orchid, pale grass, pale terra-cotta, rose red, salmon, 3 yds. each; 7mm — lt. coral, 3 yds.

Embroidery floss: lavender, lt. lavender, periwinkle, dk. periwinkle

Seed beads: #10 — bright rose, iris, mint, periwinkle, rose, violet, 1 small package each

Quilt batting: ⅓ yd.

Double-sided fusible web: ½ yd.

Fusible interfacing: 6" x 8"

Doilies: 3"-diameter, ecru (2); 6"-diameter, ecru

Tools

Glue: craft

Iron and ironing board

Needles: beading; chenille (size 20); embroidery (size 9); hand-sewing

Scissors: fabric

Sewing machine

Straight pins

Directions

•Making Patterns and Cutting Fabrics

❖Refer to General Instructions on pages 8-11.

❖Add ½" seam allowance to enlarged Bunny Body and Bunny Ear Patterns on page 28. Cut three bunny bodies from ivory moiré fabric (one right side up for lining, and two wrong side up for lining and back). Cut one bunny body from organdy fabric. Cut one bunny head from ivory moiré fabric, to middle of neck garland. Cut two bunny bodies from quilt batting. Cut two bunny ears from peach moiré fabric (for fronts). Cut two bunny ears from ivory moiré fabric (for backs). Cut two bunny ears from fusible interfacing.

•Assembling

❖Baste ivory moiré bunny head on organdy fabric bunny body, to middle of neck garland (for front).

❖Fuse scraps of fabric onto double-sided fusible web, following manufacturer's instructions. From this, cut out random shapes.

❖Arrange fabric shapes on organdy fabric, up to neck garland. Trim to fit and fuse in place.

❖With coordinating threads, machine-stitch with narrow zigzag around each fused fabric shape and around outer edges.

•Embroidery

❖Refer to General Instructions on pages 14-19. Refer to Bunny Body Transfer Sheet on page 28 and Bunny Tea Cozy Placement Diagram on page 30.

❖Embroider design onto organdy covered fabric following Ribbon Embroidery Color and Stitch Guide on page 29.

•Finishing

❖Align tracing lines on bunny body. If necessary, retrace lines and trim to fit.

❖For ears, fuse fusible interfacing to peach moiré, following manufacturer's instructions. With right sides together, pin and machine-stitch peach moiré ears to ivory moiré ears with ½" seam allowance. Trim ear points. Turn right side out and press flat. Pleat bottom edge of each ear toward the center and machine-stitch in place.

❖Pin peach side of ears to embroidered front top of bunny's head, as shown on Bunny Body Pattern on page 28. With right sides together, machine-stitch front of bunny to back of bunny with ½" seam allowance, leaving bottom of bunny open. Trim seam to ¼". Pin batting to wrong side of lining pieces. Machine-stitch both bunny body lining pieces together taking ½" seam allowance, leaving bottom of bunny open.

❖With right sides together, slip lining over embroidered bunny, lining up side seams. Machine-stitch bottom edges with ½" seam allowance, leaving bottom of bunny open. Trim seam to ¼".

❖Turn bunny right side out through opening. Top-stitch along bottom edge, closing the opening.

❖Gather-stitch through center of 6" doily to make a bow. Gather and secure thread. Using craft glue, attach doily bow to bunny's neck.

❖Make one Doily Rosette using two 3" doilies. Glue first doily to center of second doily to make rosette. Glue doily rosette to bunny's body for tail.

❖Allow glue to dry thoroughly.

Bunny Body Pattern and Transfer Sheet
Enlarge 200%

Ear placement

Bunny Ear Pattern Enlarge 200%

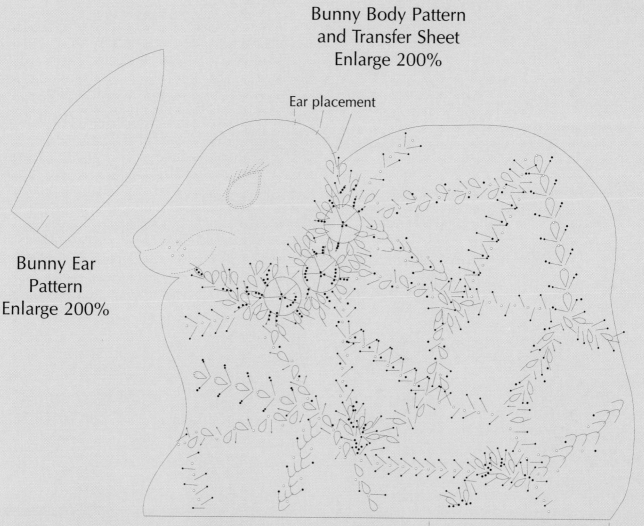

Leave open to turn

28

Bunny Tea Cozy • Ribbon Embroidery Color and Stitch Guide
Silk ribbons listed below are 4mm unless otherwise indicated.
Embroidery floss listed below is three strands unless otherwise indicated.

Bunny's Body

Step	Ribbon Color	Stitch	Step	Ribbon Color	Stitch
A1	Gray Purple	Knotted Lazy Daisy	H2	Forest Green	Ribbon Stitch
A2	Lt. Coral	Ribbon Stitch	J1	Lt. Coral	Lazy Daisy
B1	Pale Terra-Cotta	Bullion Lazy Daisy	J2	Banana	Ribbon Stitch
B2	Orchid	Ribbon Stitch	J3	Gray Purple	French Knot (1 wrap)
B3	Lichen Green	Ribbon Stitch	K1	Maroon	Bullion Lazy Daisy
C1	Pale Grass	Lazy Daisy	K2	Lavender	Ribbon Stitch
C2	Maroon	Loop Petal Stitch	K3	Lt. Avocado	Ribbon Stitch
C3	Lavender	French Knot	L1	Rose Red	French Knot (3 wraps)
D1	Glacier	Feather Stitch	L2	Lichen Green	Ribbon Stitch
D2	Salmon	French Knot	M1	Orchid	French Knot
E1	Rose Red	Ribbon Stitch	M2	Lt. Avocado	Ribbon Stitch
E2	Maroon	French Knot	N1	Lt. Avocado	Lazy Daisy
E3	Lt. Avocado	Ribbon Stitch	N2	Pale Terra-Cotta	Loop Petal Stitch
F1	Dusty Teal	Bullion Lazy Daisy	N3	Gray Purple	French Knot
F2	Dusty Purple	Loop Petal Stitch	P1	Rose Red	Ribbon Stitch
F3	Aqua	Ribbon Stitch	P2	Lichen Green	Ribbon Stitch
G1	Glacier	French Knot (3 wraps)	P3	Maroon	French Knot (1 wrap)
G2	Lt. Avocado	Ribbon Stitch	11	Beads	Beading Stitch
H1	Mauve	French Knot (3 wraps)			

Bunny's Neck Garland

Step		Ribbon Color	Stitch
1	Large Rose Centers	Salmon	Spider Web Rose
2	Large Rose Middles	Pale Terra-Cotta	Spider Web Rose
3	Large Rose Outers	Maroon	Spider Web Rose
4	Leaves	Forest Green	Bullion Lazy Daisy
5	Leaves	Lichen Green	Lazy Daisy
6	Large Petals	Lt. Coral, 7mm	Loop Petal Stitch
7	Blue Buds	Glacier	Bullion Lazy Daisy
8	Rose Buds	Maroon	Bullion Lazy Daisy
9	Leaves	Lt. Avocado	Ribbon Stitch

Bunny's Facial Features

Step		Floss Color	Stitch
1	Eye	Periwinkle	Padded Satin Stitch
2	Eye Outline, Whiskers	Lt. Lavender	Stem Stitch, French Knot
3	Outer Eye Outline	Lavender	Stem Stitch
4	Nose, Mouth	Lavender	Stem Stitch
5	Eyelashes	Dk. Periwinkle	Straight Stitch (1 strand)

Bunny Tea Cozy Placement Diagram

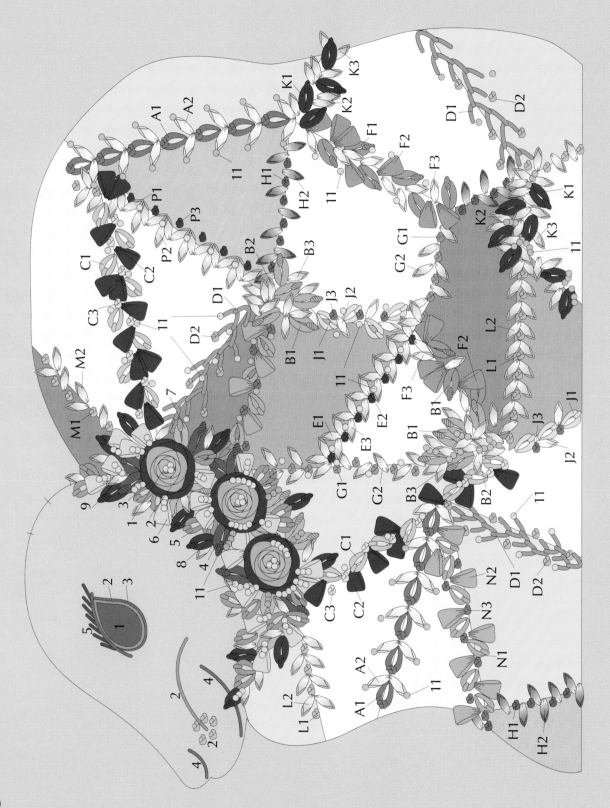

Napkin Holder

Glass - Covered Tray

Favorite Stitching

Covered Lamp

Napkin Holder

Shown on page 31.

Materials

For Each Napkin Ring

Thread: coordinating

Assorted ribbons: ⅝"-wide wired ombre, leaf shaded, ¼ yd.; 1½"-wide striped, ½ yd.; ⅝"-wide wired ombre, bright rose, ¾ yd.

Cardboard: lightweight, ½" x 7" (2)

Tools

Glue: hot glue gun and glue sticks

Needles: hand-sewing

Scissors: craft; fabric

Sewing machine

Directions

•Assembling

❖Refer to General Instructions Rolling Cardboard on page 13.

❖Using craft scissors, cut two pieces of lightweight cardboard.

❖Using a round hot glue stick, or anything similar in diameter, roll cardboard strips so each strip becomes curved. Using hot glue gun and glue stick, hot-glue strips on top of each other.

❖Fold both ends of the striped ribbon over ¼" to create finished edge. See (1).

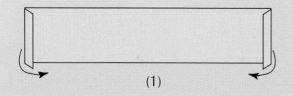

(1)

❖Fold striped ribbon in half lengthwise, matching selvages. Top-stitch across one long selvage edge and one cut edge with coordinating thread. See (2).

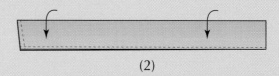

(2)

Insert cardboard into ribbon casing. Gather ribbon to fit cardboard length. Stitch or hot-glue ribbon ends closed.

❖Overlap ends ¾" and hot-glue together, to make napkin ring. See (3).

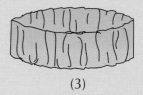

(3)

•Using Ribbons

❖Refer to General Instructions on pages 19-25.

❖Make one Double-edge Gathered Rose using bright rose wired ombre ribbon.

❖Make two Gathered Leaves using leaf shaded wired ombre ribbon. Cut into two 4½" lengths. Make one Gathered Leaf using each 4½" length.

•Finishing

❖Refer to Napkin Holder Placement Diagram below.

❖Hot-glue gathered leaves under double-edge gathered rose. Hot-glue rose cluster to napkin ring where ends overlap.

Napkin Holder Placement Diagram

Glass - Covered Tray

Shown on page 31.

Materials

Fabric: moiré, lt. green, 7" x 18"

Silk ribbons: 4mm — gray-green, taupe, 1 yd. each; dk. green, 2 yds.

Hand-dyed ribbons: 4mm — dk. green, 1 yd.; lt. green, 8 yds.; pink/rose/mauve, 11 yds.

Embroidery floss: olive green

Trim: ¼" wire metallic, ½ yd.

Beads: brass, large (4)

Frame: oval, without easel, metal, 5" x 7"

Cardboard: lightweight, 6" x 15"

Tools

Glue: craft; hot glue gun and glue sticks; industrial-strength

Needles: chenille (size 20); embroidery (sizes 3–9)

Old paintbrush or 3" paint roller

Ruler

Scissors: craft; fabric

Directions

•Making Patterns and Cutting Fabrics

❖Refer to General Instructions on pages 8-11.

❖Remove backing from frame. Using glass from frame as a pattern, make a pattern to match frame opening. Make certain fit is perfect. Using this pattern, cut two lightweight cardboard frame inserts with craft scissors (one for top and one for bottom).

❖Using fabric scissors, cut one piece of lt. green moiré fabric ½" larger than cardboard insert. Cut a second piece of lt. green moiré fabric 1" larger than cardboard insert.

•Assembling

❖Refer to General Instructions on pages 11-12.

❖Laminate ½" larger fabric around one cardboard insert to make tray bottom. Wrap extended fabric to underside.

•Embroidery

❖Refer to General Instructions on pages 14-19.

❖Embroider design onto second piece of lt. green moiré fabric following Ribbon Embroidery Color and Stitch Guide on page 34 and Glass - Covered Tray Placement Diagram below.

•Finishing

❖Using craft glue and old paintbrush or 3" paint roller, center and laminate embroidered fabric onto remaining cardboard insert. Trim excess fabric flush to edge of cardboard. Mark ⅛" in from edge of embroidered fabric and glue metallic trim on mark to make a spacer between glass and embroidered fabric.

❖Place glass, embroidered fabric (face up), and tray bottom (fabric side down) into frame. Fold frame hinges over or, if necessary, glue in place. Using industrial-strength glue, secure large brass beads on each corner of tray bottom for legs.

Glass - Covered Tray Placement Diagram

Glass - Covered Tray • Ribbon Embroidery Color and Stitch Guide

Silk ribbons listed below are 4mm unless otherwise indicated.
Embroidery floss listed below is three strands unless otherwise indicated.

Step		Ribbon and Floss Color	Stitch
1	Stems	Olive Green Floss	Stem Stitch
2	Rose Buds (Center)	Pink/Rose/Mauve (hand-dyed)	Bullion Lazy Daisy
3	Rose Buds	Pink/Rose/Mauve (hand-dyed)	Ribbon Stitch
4	Large Roses	Pink/Rose/Mauve (hand-dyed)	Ribbon Stitch
	❁Begin stitching large roses at outer petals and work inward toward center.		
5	Large Roses	Pink/Rose/Mauve (hand-dyed)	French Knot
	❁At center of top rose, stitch French Knots.		
6	Large Roses	Pink/Rose/Mauve (hand-dyed)	Fly Stitch
	❁At center of top rose, stitch Fly Stitches.		
7	Large Leaves	Lt. Green (hand-dyed)	Ribbon Stitch
8	Large Leaves	Gray-Green	Ribbon Stitch
9	Large Leaves	Gray-Green	1-Twist Ribbon Stitch
10	Calyx	Dk. Green (hand-dyed)	1-Twist Ribbon Stitch
11	Leaves, Small (2)	Dk. Green (hand-dyed)	Lazy Daisy
12	Darkest Leaves	Dk. Green	Cross-over Lazy Daisy, with Elongated Tip
	❁Stitch darkest green leaves by crossing ribbon over needle before pulling ribbon through fabric and by taking a longer tack stitch to anchor each Lazy Daisy loop.		
13	Leaves	Taupe	Bullion Lazy Daisy (2 wraps)

❁*Additional Stitch Information*

Favorite Stitching

Shown on page 31.
Materials

Fabric: homespun, ivory, 14" x 12"

Silk ribbons: 4mm — bright pink, lt. green, orchid, 1½ yds. each; bright rose, 3 yds.; bright wine, dk. dusty rose, natural white, olive green, pink, 1 yd. each; med. green, pale orchid, periwinkle, dk. periwinkle, 2 yds. each; yellow green, ½ yd.

Embroidery floss: bright rose, dk. green, lt. olive green

Tools

Needles: embroidery (size 3-9); chenille (size 20)

Scissors: fabric

Directions

•Making Patterns and Cutting Fabrics
❖Refer to General Instructions on pages 8-11.
❖Using fabric scissors, cut ivory fabric 14" x 12".

•Embroidery
❖Refer to General Instructions on pages 14-19.
❖Embroider designs randomly on ivory fabric following Ribbon Embroidery Color and Stitch Guide on pages 35-37.

Favorite Stitching • Ribbon Embroidery Color and Stitch Guide
Silk ribbons listed below are 4mm unless otherwise indicated.
Embroidery floss listed below is three strands unless otherwise indicated.

Dahlia

Step		Ribbon Color	Stitch
1	Bottom Petals	Bright Rose	Bullion Lazy Daisy
2	Petals	Bright Pink	Bullion Lazy Daisy
3	Petals	Pale Orchid	1-Twist Ribbon Stitch
4	Petals	Pink	Ribbon Stitch
5	Petals	Pink	Loop Petal Stitch

Fuchsia

Step		Ribbon and Floss Color	Stitch
1	Stems	Lt. Olive Green Floss	Stem Stitch
2	Pistils	Bright Rose Floss	Pistil Stitch
3	Fuchsia	Bright Pink	Ribbon Stitch
4	Fuchsia	Dk. Periwinkle	1-Twist Ribbon Stitch
5	Leaves	Med. Green	Bullion Lazy Daisy, Ribbon Stitch
6	Fuchsia	Dk. Periwinkle	Ribbon Stitch

Hydrangea

Step		Ribbon Color	Stitch
1	Dk. Leaves	Olive Green	Lazy Daisy
2	Petals	Bright Rose	Ribbon Stitch
3	Petals	Dk. Periwinkle	Ribbon Stitch
4	Petals	Periwinkle	Ribbon Stitch
5	Petals	Pale Orchid	Ribbon Stitch
6	Petals	Lt. Green	Ribbon Stitch

Lavender

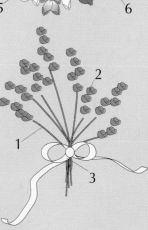

Step		Ribbon and Floss Color	Stitch
1	Stems	Lt. Olive Green Floss	Long Straight Stitch
2	Blooms	Dk. Periwinkle	French Knot
3	Bow	Pale Orchid	Tie around stems

Favorite Stitching • Ribbon Embroidery Color and Stitch Guide Continued

Silk ribbons listed below are 4mm unless otherwise indicated.
Embroidery floss listed below is three strands unless otherwise indicated.

Lilacs

Step		Ribbon and Floss Color	Stitch
1	Stems	Lt. Olive Green Floss	Stem Stitch
2	Blooms	Periwinkle	French Knot
3	Blooms	Orchid	French Knot
4	Blooms	Pale Orchid	French Knot
5	Darker Leaves	Med. Green	Long, 1-Twist Ribbon Stitch
6	Lighter Leaves	Lt. Green	Long, 1-Twist Ribbon Stitch

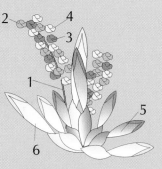

Mums

Step		Ribbon and Floss Color	Stitch
1	Stems	Lt. Olive Green Floss	Stem Stitch
2	Centers	Bright Wine	Bullion Lazy Daisy
3	Petals	Dk. Dusty Rose	1-Twist Ribbon Stitch
4	Petals	Bright Rose	1-Twist Ribbon Stitch
5	Lt. Leaves	Med. Green	Long Ribbon Stitch
6	Dk. Leaves	Olive Green	Ribbon Stitch

Pansies

Step		Ribbon and Floss Color	Stitch
1	Stems	Lt. Olive Green Floss	Stem Stitch
2	Bottom Petals	Bright Rose	Ribbon Stitch
3	Top Petals	Periwinkle	Ribbon Stitch
4	Side Petals	Dk. Periwinkle	Ribbon Stitch
5	Face	Pale Orchid	Straight Stitch
6	Dk. Leaves	Olive Green	Bullion Lazy Daisy, Ribbon Stitch
7	Lt. Leaves	Med. Green	Ribbon Stitch

Peony

Step		Ribbon Color	Stitch
1	Center	Bright Rose	Bullion Lazy Daisy
2	Petals	Dk. Dusty Rose	Twisted Ribbon Stitch, 1-Twist Ribbon Stitch
3	Petals	Bright Wine	Long Ribbon Stitch
4	Dk. Leaves	Olive Green	Lazy Daisy
5	Lt. Leaves	Med. Green	Ribbon Stitch

Favorite Stitching • Ribbon Embroidery Color and Stitch Guide

Silk ribbons listed below are 4mm unless otherwise indicated.
Embroidery floss listed below is three strands unless otherwise indicated.

Queen Anne's Lace

Step		Ribbon and Floss Color	Stitch
1	Stems	Lt. Olive Green Floss	Stem Stitch
2	Blooms	Natural White	French Knot
3	Leaves	Lt. Green	Ribbon Stitch
4	Leaves	Yellow Green	Ribbon Stitch
5	Leaves	Lt. Green	Ribbon Stitch

Rose Bud Spray

Step		Ribbon and Floss Color	Stitch
1	Stems	Lt. Olive Green Floss	Stem Stitch
2	Rose Buds	Bright Rose	Bullion Lazy Daisy
3	Rose Petals	Bright Wine	Ribbon Stitch
4	Light Leaves	Med. Green	Ribbon Stitch
5	Dark Leaves	Olive Green	Ribbon Stitch

Rose Spray

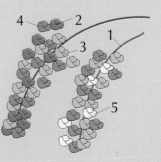

Step		Ribbon and Floss Color	Stitch
1	Stems	Dk. Green Floss	Stem Stitch
2	Rose Center, bud	Bright Rose	Bullion Lazy Daisy
3	Rose Petals	Bright Wine	Ribbon Stitch
4	Rose Petals	Bright Rose	Ribbon Stitch
5	Lt. Leaves	Med. Green	Ribbon Stitch
6	Dk. Leaves	Olive Green	Ribbon Stitch

Wisteria

Step		Ribbon and Floss Color	Stitch
1	Stems	Lt. Olive Green Floss	Stem Stitch
2	Blooms	Dk. Periwinkle	French Knot
3	Blooms	Periwinkle	French Knot
4	Blooms	Orchid	French Knot
5	Blooms	Pale Orchid	French Knot

Covered Lamp

Shown on page 31.
Materials

Assorted ribbons: 1½"-wide metallic, sheer mauve, ¾ yd. each

Embroidered lace or eyelet: 2"-wide natural white or vintage, ¾ yd.

Trim: ½"-wide braided, ivory, ½ yd.

Doilies: 6"-diameter, natural white or vintage; 8"-diameter, natural white or vintage

Pansies: velvet, violet (2)

Flower/leaf spray: pale lavender

Candlestick lamp: metal or cloth shade, small

Tools

Glue: craft, thin-bodied; hot glue gun and glue sticks

Old paintbrush

Scissors: craft; fabric

shade as possible. Trim doily at top edge of lampshade, ½" above rim.

❖Drape and glue 8" doily around lampshade so doily evenly curves around to front side of 6" doily. Trim doily at top edge of lampshade, ½" below rim. Fold this ½" excess doily to inside of lampshade and glue.

•Finishing

❖Tie a bow around top of candlestick, just below lampshade, with metallic ribbon. Using hot glue gun and glue sticks, hot-glue center of bow to candlestick. Cascade ribbon ends down and hot-glue in place.

❖Using craft scissors, cut flower/leaf spray apart. Hot-glue one pansy, three pale lavender flowers, and three leaves around candlestick on top of lamp base. Hot-glue three pale lavender flowers and two leaves to top front edge of lampshade where doilies meet. Hot-glue remaining pansy, one pale lavender flower, and two leaves to candlestick where ribbon ends are hot glued in place.

Directions

•Assembling

❖Refer to General Instructions on pages 8-11.

❖Using old paintbrush, apply thin-bodied craft glue to candlestick portion of lamp. Carefully wrap embroidered lace around candlestick. Leave ¼" space between spiraling lace.

❖Glue lace, diagonally, onto lamp base, gathering lace at corners. Using fabric scissors, trim lace flush to edge of lamp base. Using hot glue gun and glue stick, hot-glue ivory braided trim around bottom edge of lamp base.

❖Evenly drape and glue 6" doily around lampshade so doily covers as much of one side of

Additional Design for Lampshade

Woven Sachets

Crocheted Doily Sachets

Satin Sachets

Bookmark

Woven Sachets

Shown on page 39.

Materials

For Pencil Violet Sachet

Silk ribbons: 4mm — blush, ¾ yd.; lavender, ⅜ yd.; 7mm — dusty lavender, ⅜ yd.; palest peach, ¾ yd.

For Fuchsia Sachet

Embroidery floss or narrow cording: ecru, for stems

Assorted ribbon: 1½"-wide ombre, pale rose/green, ⅓ yd.

Stamens: small

For Each Sachet

Fabrics: coordinating fabric, 7" x 4½", for pocket potpourri-enclosure fabric, 4" x 6"

Thread: coordinating

Assorted ribbons: ⅜"-wide grosgrain, two coordinating colors, 1⅛ yds.; ⅛"-wide metallic (or grosgrain), gold, ⅝ yd.; ¼"-wide satin, coordinating color, ½ yd., for ribbon hanger

Double-sided fusible web: 3" x 3" square

Cardboard box: small

Potpourri

Tools

Glue: of choice

Iron and ironing board

Needles: hand-sewing; large-eyed

Pencils: (2)

Ruler

Scissors: craft; fabric

Snaps: (2)

Sewing machine

Straight pins

Directions

•Making Patterns and Cutting Fabrics

❖Refer to General Instructions on pages 8-11.

❖Using pencil and ruler, draw a 4" x 3¼" rectangle onto cardboard box side.

•Assembling

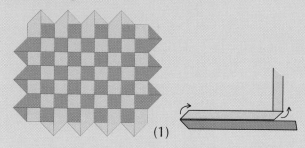

(1)

❖Beginning at right bottom corner of cardboard, pin first shade of grosgrain ribbon to bottom edge of traced rectangle, allowing a 1¼" ribbon extension past right edge. Extend ribbon across rectangle to left bottom corner of cardboard and pin. At left edge, turn grosgrain ribbon under at a 45° angle. See (1). Pin fold to cardboard. Turn ribbon forward at 45° angle. Pin fold to cardboard. Extend ribbon across rectangle to right edge, butting ribbon edges up to each other. Fold ribbon under 45° and forward 45°, as in first row, pinning folds to cardboard. Continue to cover traced rectangle with ribbon, folding it at each end and pinning to cardboard. End ribbon at top left edge with ribbon extending 1¼" past traced edge.

❖Using large-eyed needle and beginning at bottom left corner, weave second shade of grosgrain ribbon through first shade, lining edge of second shade up to left edge of traced rectangle. Extend ribbon 1¼" past bottom left corner. At top edge, turn ribbon down 45°, and then forward 45°, as was done with first shade. Pin to cardboard. Continue to weave and fold ribbon until second shade is completely woven through first shade. Extend ribbon 1¼" past top right corner for last row. Remove all pins from cardboard. Tuck under extended ribbons while pressing the woven piece with iron.

❖Fuse underside of woven ribbon onto fusible web, following manufacturer's instructions.

❖Press sachet pocket fabric down ½" at each 4½" edge. Fold fabric in half, right sides together, lining up 4½" edges. Stitch a ¼" seam at sides, leaving folded-down edge open. See (2). Turn right side out. Press.

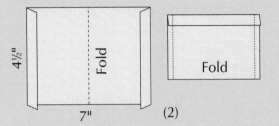

(2)

❖Fuse woven ribbon sides to sachet pocket. Tack a snap to top folded edge of pocket for easy potpourri removal.

❖Fold ¼"-wide satin ribbon in half lengthwise. Tie knot ¾" from fold. See (3). Fold ends into two loops. See (4). Tack ends. See (5). Glue ribbon hanger to outside top front corners of sachet at ribbon loops.

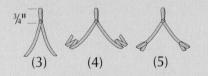

(3)   (4)   (5)

❖At center of ⅛" wide ribbon, tack a small 6-looped bow. Tack or glue small bow to top knot of satin ribbon hanger. Drape and secure ribbon ends to satin loops at front sachet corners.

•**Using Ribbons**

❖Refer to General Instructions on pages 19-25.

❖Refer to Pencil Violet Sachet Placement Diagram. Make two Pencil Violets using 4mm blush ribbon. Make one Pencil Violet using 4mm lavender ribbon. Make one Pencil Violet using 7mm dusty lavender ribbon. Make two Pencil

Violets using 7mm palest peach ribbon. Glue or tack violets to sachet pad front.

❖Refer to Fuchsia Sachet Placement Diagram. Make three Fuchsias using ombre pale rose/green ribbon. Cut ribbon into three 4" pieces. Cut three 6" lengths of floss or narrow cording for fuchsia stems. Glue stamens to inside center of fuchsia. Glue or tack fuchsias to sachet pad front.

•**Finishing**

❖With right sides together, fold potpourri-enclosure fabric in half. Machine-stitch ends. Turn right side out. Fill with favorite potpourri. Turn under and hand-stitch top closed. Slip into sachet pocket. Replace sachet enclosure when necessary.

Pencil Violet Sachet Placement Diagram

Fuchsia Sachet Placement Diagram

Crocheted Doily Sachets

Shown on page 39.

Materials

For Large Sachet

Fabric: lining, 9" x 18"

Thread: coordinating

Cording: narrow, white, 1¼ yds.

Doilies: 1½"-diameter, small flower shape, white (7); 2½"-diameter, small flower shape, white (7); 3"-diameter, small flower shape, white (1); 10"-diameter, crocheted, white (2)

Acrylic paint: pale yellow; pale rose

For Small Sachet

Fabric: lining, 6" x 12"

Thread: coordinating

Cording: narrow, mauve, ⅞ yd.

Doilies: 1½"-diameter, small flower shape, ecru (6); 2¼"-diameter, small flower shape, ecru (2); 6"-diameter, crocheted, ecru (2)

Acrylic paint: old rose

Velvet leaves: rose/brown (2)

Tools

Cotton swabs

Paint dish: disposable

Glue: hot glue gun and glue sticks

Iron and ironing board

Scissors: fabric

Sewing machine

Straight pins

Textile medium

Directions

For Large Sachet

•Making Patterns and Cutting Fabrics

❖Refer to General Instructions on pages 8-11.

❖Add ¼" seam allowance to Large Sachet Bag Lining Pattern on page 43. Using fabric scissors, cut two large sachet bag linings from lining fabric.

•Assembling and Using Ribbons

❖Refer to General Instructions on pages 14 and 19-25.

❖Use pale yellow and pale rose acrylic paint. Paint centers of five 2½" doilies and five 1½" doilies.

❖Make one Doily Rosette by hot-gluing one 1½" doily in center of one 2½" doily. Repeat this process for a total of five doily rosettes for bottom edge of sachet.

❖Paint centers of one 3" doily, two 1½" doilies, and two 2¼" doilies.

❖Make one large Doily Rosette by hot-gluing 1½" folded doilies in centers of two 2¼" doilies, then hot-gluing both into 3" doily.

❖Fold edge of each 10" doily down 4". See (1) on page 43.

❖Pin and machine-stitch curved edges of doilies together at outer edge with narrow zigzag. Machine-topstitch around top folded edges as close to fold as possible. Machine-topstitch again ½" away from first stitching to create casing. See (2) on page 43.

❖Machine-stitch sachet bag lining pieces together with ¼" seam, leaving top edge open. Turn down top edge ½" onto right side of lining. Press. Pin and stitch lining to inside top edge of doily bag just below second row of stitching. Be careful not to catch bag flap when stitching.

•Finishing

❖Cut cording in half. Insert cording through left side casing opening. Tie ends of cording together, then move cording so knot is hidden within casing. Repeat for right side casing.

❖Refer to Crocheted Doily Sachet Placement Diagram below. Hot-glue five doily rosettes to bottom edge of sachet bag. Hot-glue large doily rosette at center top edge.

❖Fill with favorite sachet. Pull on drawstring cords to close. Replace sachet when necessary.

Directions

For Small Sachet

•Making Patterns and Cutting Fabrics

❖Refer to General Instructions on pages 8-11.

❖Add ¼" seam allowance to Small Sachet Bag Lining Pattern below. Using fabric scissors, cut two small sachet bag linings from lining fabric.

•Assembling and Using Ribbons

❖Refer to General Instructions on pages 14 and 19-25.

❖Use old rose acrylic paint. Paint center of five 1½" doilies.

❖Make one Doily Rosette using 1½" doily. Place a thin bead of glue in center of doily. Fold doily up around glue, gathering so doily ruffles slightly.

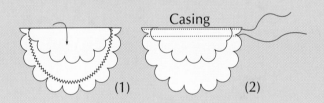

(1)   Casing   (2)

Repeat this process for a total of five doily rosettes for bottom edge of sachet.

❖Paint the center of one 2¼" doily.

❖Make one large Doily Rosette by hot-gluing one 1½" doily in center of 2¼" doily. Hot-glue these to the center of second 2¼".

❖For sachet lining, fold edge of 6" doily down 2". See (1).

❖Pin and machine-stitch curved edges of 6" doilies together at outer edge with a narrow zigzag. Machine-topstitch around top folded edges as close to fold as possible. Machine-topstitch again ½" away from first stitching to create a casing. See (2).

❖Machine-stitch sachet bag lining pieces together with ¼" seam, leaving top edge open. Turn down top edge ½" onto right side of lining. Press. Pin and stitch lining to inside top edge of doily bag just below second row of stitching. Be careful not to catch bag flap when stitching.

•Finishing

❖Cut cording in half. Insert cording through left side casing opening. Tie ends of cording together, then move cording so knot is hidden within casing. Repeat for right side casing.

❖Refer to Crocheted Doily Sachet Placement Diagram below. Hot-glue five doily rosettes to bottom edge of sachet bag. Hot-glue large doily rosette at center top edge. Hot-glue velvet leaves underneath top edge of large doily rosette.

❖Fill with favorite sachet. Pull on drawstring cords to close. Replace sachet when necessary.

Turn down here

Sachet Lining Pattern
Small — Enlarge 170%
Large — Enlarge 215%

Crocheted Doily Sachet Placement Diagram

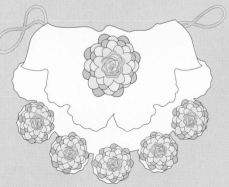

Satin Sachets

Shown on page 39.

Materials

For Each Sachet

Fabric: satin, 6" x 12"

Thread: coordinating

Assorted ribbons: ⅞" to 1½"-wide fancy, ½ yd.;
   1½"-wide sheer, ¾ yd.

Beads: gold, small (2); silver, large (2)

Stuffing: polyester

Potpourri

Tools

Glue: of choice

Needles: hand-sewing

Ruler

Scissors: fabric

Straight pins

Sewing machine

Directions

•Making Patterns and Cutting Fabrics

❖Refer to General Instructions on pages 8-11.

❖Using fabric scissors, cut two 3" x 12" lengths from satin fabric. Cut fancy ribbon into two 7" lengths.

•Assembling

❖Align two fancy ribbon lengths lengthwise and machine-stitch together with a narrow zigzag.

❖On each length of satin fabric, machine-gather-stitch down one 12" side, ¼" from edge. Machine-stitch a second row of gather stitches, ⅛" away from first row. Repeat for second strip.

❖Adjust gathering stitches on satin strip to fit one finished edge of ribbon. Overlap finished edge of ribbon onto gathered edge of fabric and pin. Using narrow zigzag, machine-stitch satin in place, finished edge to overlap raw edge. Repeat for second satin strip.

❖Fold ribbon and satin in half, matching short raw ends. Machine-stitch ½" seam. Finger-press seam open. Turn right side out.

❖Turn one raw edge of satin strip under ¼" while hand-gather-stitching. Tightly gather and secure thread, forming a tube.

❖Stuff tube firmly with stuffing and potpourri mixture. Turn under remaining raw edge of satin strip ¼" while hand-gather-stitching. Tightly gather and secure thread.

•Finishing

❖Refer to General Instructions on pages 14-25.

❖Using a Beading Stitch, stitch beads to each end of one sachet.

❖For second sachet, make two Gathered Rosebuds using 1½"-wide sheer ribbon. Cut two 13½" lengths. Fold each length of ribbon in half matching selvages before stitching gathered rosebud. Glue one gathered rosebud to each end of sachet.

Additional Design for Satin Sachet

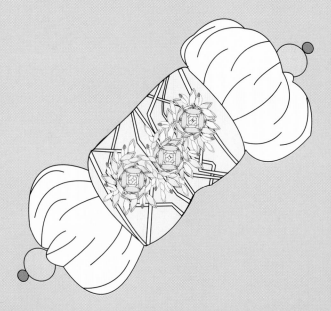

Bookmark

Shown on page 39.
Materials

Thread: coordinating

Silk ribbons: 4mm — blush, gray, ivory, pale peach, taupe, 1¼ yds. each

Assorted ribbons: ½"-wide grosgrain, tan, ½ yd.; ½"-wide, pale green, ½ yd.

Lace: ¾"-wide Swiss embroidery insertion, ½ yd., allow ¼" for seam allowance; 1"-wide Swiss embroidery, ⅞ yd.

Tools

Glue: hot glue gun and glue sticks

Iron and ironing board

Needles: hand-sewing

Ruler

Scissors: fabric

Sewing machine

Directions

•Making Patterns and Cutting Fabrics

❖Refer to General Instructions on pages 8-11.

❖Using fabric scissors, cut 1"-wide Swiss embroidery lace into two equal lengths.

•Assembling

❖With right sides together, machine-stitch using a narrow zigzag Swiss embroidery lace to Swiss insertion lace. Trim seam to ¹⁄₁₆". Press seam toward insertion. Stitch 1"-wide lace to opposite edge of insertion lace. Trim seam to ¹⁄₁₆". Press seam toward insertion.

❖Fold top edge of lace down 1½" to backside of bookmark. Gather-stitch across lace 1" from folded edge. Tightly gather and secure thread.

❖With right sides together, fold bottom edge of lace in half. Diagonally stitch across lace. See (1). Trim seam to ⅛". Turn point right side out. Press.

❖Cut 18" each from all five shades of 4mm silk ribbon. Hold the five shades of silk ribbon together. Fold ribbons into a 3"-wide, ten-looped bow, having 11" tails on one side only. Gather-stitch across center of bow. Tightly gather and secure thread. Refer to Placement Diagram below. Hot-glue bow center to bookmark front at gathered center. Knot ribbon ends.

•Using Ribbons

❖Refer to General Instructions on pages 19-25. Refer to Bookmark Placement Diagram below.

❖Make one Rosette using ½"-wide tan grosgrain ribbon. Cut one 6" length.

❖Make two Folded Leaves using ½"-wide pale green grosgrain ribbon. Cut two 9" lengths. Hot-glue leaves to underside of rosette on left side. Hot-glue rosette over bow center.

❖Make one Rosette using 4mm taupe ribbon. Cut one 5" length.

❖Hold remaining silk ribbons together. Measure 7" from ends. Drape ribbon into a 5" deep loop at 7" mark. Gather-stitch across ribbons at top fold to hold all in place. Hot-glue gathered edge to underside of bookmark at center bottom point.

•Finishing

❖Hot-glue rosette to front of bookmark at center bottom point. Knot ribbon ends.

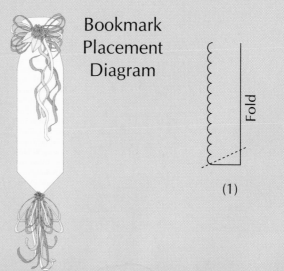

Bookmark Placement Diagram

Fold

(1)

Hankie Holder

Hankie Holder

Materials

Fabrics: moiré, lt. taupe, 9" x 18"; sheer, ecru, 9" x 18"; natural white, 9" x 18"

Thread: coordinating

Silk ribbons: 4mm — heather, ivory, pale orchid, pale peach, pale periwinkle, pale yellow, 2 yds. each; 7mm — pale yellow, 1 yd.

Assorted ribbon: 2"-wide grosgrain, ivory, ¼ yd.

Lace: 1"-wide, 1½ yds.; 2"-wide, ½ yd.

Trim: 1"-wide scalloped, natural white, 1 yd.; 2½"-wide scalloped, natural white, ¼ yd.

Quilt batting: 9" x 7"

Doily: 4" or 5"-diameter, with a center suitable for embroidery

Cardboard: lightweight, 7" square (2); 6⅞" square (2); 3" square for heart pattern

Tools

Glue: hot glue gun and glue sticks

Needles: chenille (size 20); hand-sewing

Straight pins

Ruler

Scissors: craft; fabric

Directions

•Making Patterns and Cutting Fabrics

❖Refer to General Instructions on pages 8-11.

❖Using fabric scissors, cut two 9" squares from moiré fabric (for front outside and back outside pieces).

❖Cut two 9" squares from sheer fabric (to go on top of moiré for front outside and back outside pieces).

❖Cut two 9" squares from natural fabric (for front inside and back inside pieces).

❖Using craft scissors, cut one heart from cardboard using Hankie Holder Heart Pattern on page 49.

•Embroidery

❖Refer to General Instructions on pages 14-19.

❖Refer to Transfer Sheet and Placement Diagram on page 49. Embroider design to center of doily following Ribbon Embroidery Color and Stitch Guide on page 49.

•Assembling

❖Refer to General Instructions on pages 11-14.

❖Pad one 7" square piece of cardboard with batting. Trim batting flush to cardboard's edge and bevel inward slightly.

❖Using hot glue gun and glue sticks, snugly wrap and hot-glue padded cardboard with moiré fabric. Wrap and hot-glue sheer fabric around moiré fabric. Trim bulk from corners.

❖Wrap and hot-glue remaining 7" piece of cardboard with moiré and sheer fabric (for back outside piece). This piece is not padded with quilt batting.

❖Pad cardboard heart with batting trimmed flush to edge. Slip padded heart underneath embroidered doily center.

❖Center and pin embroidered doily to front. Hand-stitch doily to padded cardboard at outer edge of padded heart to tuft doily. Hand-stitch outer edge of doily to front.

❖Wrap 2½"-wide scalloped trim around bottom corners of front. Hot-glue 1"-wide scalloped trim to underside edge of front.

❖Hot-glue 1"-wide lace to underside edge of back, gathering lace at corners only.

❖Cut 7mm pale yellow ribbon into two 18" pieces. Mark center of one edge of padded cardboard back. This becomes the front edge. Hot-glue end of 7mm ribbon onto center mark on underside. Mark center of front where heart point faces and hot-glue ribbon in place.

❖Wrap each 6⅞" piece of cardboard with natural white fabric. Trim bulk from corners. These are the inside liners. Glue 2"-wide lace around each wrapped cardboard, 1" in from all edges. These become the front edge.

❖For the ribbon hinge, cut 2"-wide ribbon into two 3" pieces. Hot-glue long edge of ribbons to back edge of inside back on underside.

•Finishing

❖ With wrong sides together, center and hot-glue the hinged liner to back. With right sides together, place remaining liner on top of back liner. Hot-glue ribbon tabs onto back side of remaining liner. With wrong sides together, hot-glue front liner to front. Tie silk ribbons to close.

Hankie Holder

Hankie Holder • Ribbon Embroidery Color and Stitch Guide

Silk ribbons listed below are 4mm unless otherwise indicated.

Step		Ribbon Color	Stitch
1	Roses	Pale Peach, Pale Yellow, Ivory	Ruffled Ribbon Stitch
	✪For larger roses, stitch several Ruffled Ribbon Stitches to form a circular petal cluster. For smaller roses, stitch one ruffle ribbon stitch. To create a full bloom, overlap Ruffled Ribbon Stitches around centers of larger roses.		
2	Petals	Pale Periwinkle	Loop Petal Stitch
3	Petals	Pale Orchid	1-Twist Ribbon Stitch
4	Petals	Heather	Ribbon Stitch
5	Multi-loop Bow	Pale Yellow, Pale Periwinkle	
	✪Cut 18" of each ribbon. Stitch knot of bow in place.		
6	Bow Tail	Pale Yellow Pale Periwinkle	Cascade Stitch

✪*Additional Stitch Information*

Hankie Holder Placement Diagram

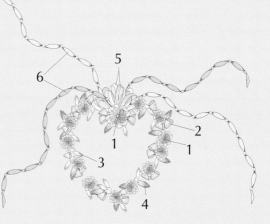

Hankie Holder Transfer Sheet
Enlarge 155%

Hankie Holder Heart Pattern
Enlarge 155%

49

Journal Cover

Note Cards

Letter Holder

Love Letter Box

Journal Cover

Materials

Fabrics: print with tan background, ⅓ yd.; ecru or ivory organdy, organza, or voile, ⅓ yd.

Thread: coordinating

Silk ribbons: 4mm — blush, gray-green, pale green, pale peach, rose, tan, 1½ yds. each; 7mm — ivory, pale green, 1½ yds. each

Assorted ribbon: ½"-wide grosgrain, tan, ½ yd.

Lace: ½"-wide French Valenciennes, 1 yd.

Cording: narrow, ecru or ivory, 1 yd.

Quilt batting: 11" x 9"

Doilies: 6"-diameter, ecru or ivory (2)

Journal: 5½" x 8½"

Cardboard: lightweight, 10" x 17"

Tools

Glue: hot glue gun and glue sticks; craft, thin-bodied

Old paintbrush

Iron and ironing board

Needles: chenille (size 20); hand-sewing

Scissors: craft; fabric

Sewing machine

Directions

•Making Patterns and Cutting Fabrics

❖Refer to General Instructions on pages 8-11.

❖Using craft scissors, cut cardboard into two 5" x 8½" pieces. (For a different size journal, cut cardboard pieces same height as book front and ½" less in width.)

❖Using fabric scissors, cut four pieces of print fabric and four pieces of organdy, organza, or voile fabric ¾" larger than cardboard pieces.

❖Cut one 2½" x 10" strip of print fabric and one 2½" x 10" strip of organdy, organza, or voile fabric.

•Assembling

❖Refer to General Instructions on pages 11-12.

❖Gently pull book pages away from binding along spine. Using thin-bodied craft glue and old paintbrush, center and glue 2½" x 10 " print fabric strip over outside book spine. Fold ends over at top and bottom and glue to inside. Lay one 2½" x 10" organdy, organza, or voile fabric strip over print fabric strip and glue at long edges. Fold ends over at top and bottom and glue to inside. Close book and let glue dry thoroughly, allowing pulled away pages to be glued back in place.

❖Layer each organdy, organza, or voile fabric piece over each print fabric piece. Machine- or baste-stitch together at edges.

❖To line inside of book, fold back ¾" along one long side of one piece of layered fabric. Press. Repeat on second piece. Position one piece over book inside front placing folded edge toward spine. Wrap and glue raw edges of fabric around to outside of book. Trim bulk from corners. Repeat to line back.

❖Pad both pieces of cardboard with batting. Trim batting flush to cardboard's edge and bevel inward slightly.

❖For journal back, tightly wrap one piece of layered fabric onto one cardboard piece. Trim bulk from corners.

•Embroidery

❖Refer to General Instructions on pages 14-25.

❖Embroider design onto remaining piece of layered fabric for journal front following Ribbon Embroidery and Flower Work Color and Stitch Guide on page 52. Refer to Placement Diagram on page 52.

•Finishing

❖Tightly wrap embroidered fabric around remaining padded cardboard. Wrap portion of doily around bottom right corner of journal front. Hot-glue edges to underside. Cut remaining doily in half. Wrap and hot-glue one piece around bottom left corner and one piece around top right corner of journal.

❖Using hot glue gun and glue stick, hot-glue padded back to journal back. Hot-glue narrow cording to gully between wrapped cardboard and book.

❖Hot-glue edge of lace to underside edge of padded front, gathering lace at corners. Hot-glue padded front to journal front.

Journal Cover • Ribbon Embroidery and Flower Work Color and Stitch Guide

Silk ribbons listed below are 4mm unless otherwise indicated.

Step		Ribbon Color	Stitch and Flower Stitch
1	Largest Petals	Ivory, 7mm	Lazy Daisy
2	Clustered Petals	Pale Peach	1-Twist Ribbon Stitch
3	Clustered Petals	Blush	1-Twist Ribbon Stitch
4	Clustered Petals	Tan	1-Twist Ribbon Stitch
5	Leaves	Gray-Green	Ribbon Stitch
6	Bow Tail	Rose	Cascade Stitch
	✿Cut ribbon into 24" length. Stitch a 2"-wide, four-looped bow at center of cut length. Stitch knot of bow to center top of rosette cluster. Cascade stitch ribbon ends.		
7	Buds	Blush	Lazy Daisy
8	Rosette	½"-Wide Tan Grosgrain	Rosette
	✿Cut ribbon into 18" length.		
9	Leaves	Pale Green	Ribbon Stitch
10	Leaves	Pale Green, 7mm	Folded Leaf
	✿Cut ribbon into two 9" lengths. Make two folded leaves.		

✿*Additional Stitch Information*

Journal Cover Placement Diagram

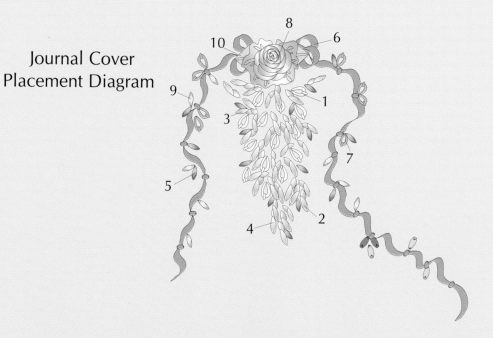

52

Note Cards

Shown on page 50.

Materials

For Each Note Card

Silk ribbons: 7mm — ivory, pale peach or taupe, ⅜ yd. each

Lace: delicate, 6¼" x 4¼"; 1¼"-wide galloon, ¼ yd.

Sketch paper

Tools

Glue: glue stick; hot glue gun and glue sticks

Scissors: fabric

Directions

•Making Patterns and Cutting Fabrics

❖Refer to General Instructions on pages 8-11.

❖Using fabric scissors, cut sketch paper 6½" x 9" for each note card. Fold in half so front measures 6½" x 4½".

•Assembling

❖Using a glue stick, attach 6¼" x 4¼" lace to front of each note card.

❖Glue galloon lace to bottom front edge of each note card.

•Using Ribbons

❖Refer to General Instructions on page 23-24.

❖Make one Pencil Violet using 7mm ivory ribbon and one using 7mm pale peach or taupe ribbon.

•Finishing

❖Using hot glue gun and glue stick, hot-glue knot of each pencil violet to center top edge of galloon lace of each note card. Drape ribbon ends and hot-glue in place.

Letter Holder

Shown on page 50.

Materials

Fabrics: moiré faille, terra-cotta, 9" x 14"; velveteen, hunter green, 9" x 21"

Thread: coordinating

Silk ribbons: 4mm — blue green, blush, hunter green, lt. taupe, olive green, ¾ yd. each

Assorted ribbon: ¼"-wide velvet, hunter green, 1 yd.

Embroidery floss: olive green, med. olive green, pale peach

Cording: narrow, hunter green, ⅜ yd.

Quilt batting: 6" x 5"

Charms, antique brass: large cameo; filigree half-circles (2); standing cupid (2); fan shape (2); floral swag; flourishes (2)

Cardboard: heavy, 9" x 32"

Tools

Glue: craft, thin-bodied; hot glue gun and glue sticks; industrial-strength

Old paintbrush or 3" paint roller

Needles: chenille (size 20); hand-sewing; milliner's

Ruler

Scissors: craft; fabric

Utility knife

Directions

•Making Patterns and Cutting Fabrics

❖Refer to General Instructions on pages 8-13.

❖See Letter Holder Patterns on pages 55-56. Using craft scissors, cut two each of letter holder back and front, one pedestal, one base, and five spacer pieces from cardboard. Using ruler and utility knife, mark and cut score lines on pedestal where indicated.

❖Add ¾" seam allowance. Using fabric scissors, cut one back, one front, one pedestal, and one base from velveteen fabric (for inside pieces), using cardboard pieces as patterns.

❖Adding 1" seam allowance, cut one spacer from velveteen fabric, using one cardboard spacer as pattern.

❖Adding ¾" seam allowance, cut one back and one front from moiré fabric (for outside pieces), using cardboard pieces as patterns.

❖Place and label fabric cuts with corresponding cardboard pieces.

•Assembling

❖Refer to General Instructions on pages 11-13.

❖Using thin-bodied craft glue and old paintbrush or 3" paint roller, layer and glue five spacer pieces together.

❖Laminate velveteen fabric to cardboard pieces for back, front, and base. Trim bulk from corners.

❖Repeat process with moiré fabric and cardboard piece for back. Trim bulk from corners.

❖Center and glue spacer cardboard onto spacer fabric. At long edges, wrap extending fabric around to underside. At short edges, cut velveteen fabric flush to top side edge. Turn fabric under at long edge of spacer to create a finished tab edge. This turned-under fabric will overlap at center, creating bulk. Trim overlap so turned-under fabric is only ¼" wide. Glue tab around short edge to underside of spacer.

❖With scored side down, center and glue cardboard pedestal onto pedestal fabric. Wrap extending fabric onto opposite side of cardboard. Cut into corners. Wrap long edge to underside only at corners.

•Embroidery

❖Refer to General Instructions on pages 14-19.

❖Refer to Placement Diagram on page 56. Embroider design onto front of moiré fabric, following Ribbon Embroidery Color and Stitch Guide on page 55.

•Finishing

❖Refer to General Instructions on pages 11-13 and 15.

❖Pad front cardboard with batting. Trim batting flush to cardboard's edge and bevel inward slightly.

❖Tightly wrap embroidered front fabric around padded front. Trim bulk from corners.

❖Fold pedestal on score lines. Glue corners of pedestal together on underside. On top side, trim extended velveteen at short edges flush to corner for clean finish.

❖Flute while gluing ¼"-wide hunter green ribbon to underside of base so fluting extends ¹⁄₁₆" from base edge. With wrong sides together, glue base to pedestal.

❖With wrong sides together, glue letter holder velveteen back to moiré back. Glue one long side edge of spacer to bottom edge of letter holder back on velveteen side.

❖Using industrial-strength glue, attach large brass cameo to center top of letter holder back on velveteen side. Let glue dry thoroughly.

❖Position charms around letter holder front. With coordinating thread, secure charms to front outer edge of letter holder, stitching through cardboard, if necessary. Use industrial-strength glue to attach brass pieces that cannot be stitched to letter holder front. Let glue dry thoroughly.

❖With wrong sides together, using thin-bodied craft glue, glue letter holder velveteen front to moiré front.

❖Carefully glue narrow cording between the two fronts to fill gap.

❖Glue remaining long side edge of spacer to bottom edge of letter holder front on velveteen side.

❖Flute while gluing hunter green velvet ribbon to underside of assembled letter holder so fluting extends ⅛" from bottom edge.

❖Glue letter holder to pedestal.

Letter Holder • Ribbon Embroidery Color and Stitch Guide
Silk ribbons listed below are 4mm unless otherwise indicated.
Embroidery floss listed below is three strands unless otherwise indicated.

Step		Ribbon and Floss Color	Stitch
1	Stems	Olive Green Floss	Straight Stitch
2	Stem Crossbars	Med. Olive Green Floss	Straight Stitch
3	Roses	Blush	Ruffled Ribbon Stitch
	❂Stitch rose centers with Ruffled Ribbon Stitches clustered in a circle.		
4	Roses	Lt. Taupe	Ruffled Ribbon Stitch
	❂Stitch outer edge of roses with Ruffled Ribbon Stitches placed around centers.		
5	Leaves	Olive Green	Lazy Daisy
6	Leaves	Hunter Green	Ribbon Stitch
7	Bullions	Pale Peach Floss	Bullion Stitch (7-8 wraps)
8	Leaves	Blue Green	Ribbon Stitch

❂*Additional Stitch Information*

Letter Holder Patterns
Enlarge 250%

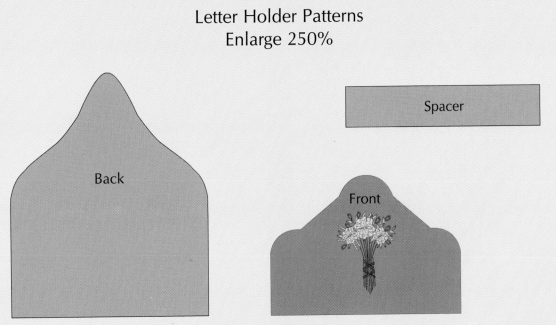

Spacer

Back

Front

Letter Holder Patterns
Enlarge 140%

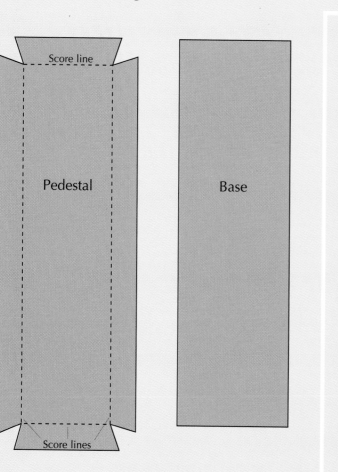

Letter Holder
Placement Diagram

Love Letter Box

Shown on page 50.

Materials

Fabrics: outer fabric, ½ yd.; inside coordinating fabric, ⅓ yd.

Thread: coordinating

Silk ribbon: 7mm — pale peach, ¼ yd.

Assorted ribbons: ¼"-wide, velvet, peach, 1⅓ yds.; ½"-wide, stripe, rose, 1⅛ yds.; ½"-wide, grosgrain, pale peach, ½ yd.; ⅝"-wide, grosgrain, peach, ⅓ yd.

Cording: narrow, peach/gold, 1 yd.

Charms: brass (2)

Cardboard: lightweight, 30" x 20"

Papier mâché box: treasure chest-shaped

Tools

Glue: craft, thin-bodied; hot glue gun and glue sticks; industrial-strength

Old paintbrush or 3" paint roller

Needles: chenille (size 20); hand-sewing; milliner's

Ruler

Scissors: craft; fabric

Directions

•Making Patterns and Cutting Fabrics

❖Refer to General Instructions on pages 8-11.

❖For box top, using fabric scissors, cut fabric 2" larger than box top measures from front to back and as wide as box top measures across top and down each side. See (1) and (2).

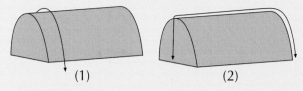

(1) (2)

•Assembling

❖Refer to General Instructions on pages 11-12 and 20.

❖Using thin-bodied craft glue and 3" paint roller, laminate box top. Do not glue box top sides. Place and smooth fabric onto box top, centered over glued area. At front and back edge, glue and wrap extending fabric to inside of box top. Trim fabric at corners. See (3).

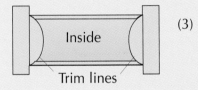

Inside

(3)

Trim lines

❖Glue and wrap extending fabric around to box side. Trim fabric to overlap slightly at side center. Glue and wrap fabric that is extending past side bottom edge to box inside. Trim fabric on inside corners for clean finish.

❖Finger-pleat remaining fabric on box side so it lies flat against box side. Glue pleats to box side ½" from bottom edge. Trim fabric at bottom edge if necessary. See (4).

(4)

❖Cut fabric strip 1½" wider than box bottom height and the same length as box, plus ½". Glue fabric onto box side so long edges extend ¾" past top and bottom edges. Glue extended top fabric to top box inside, cutting corners as necessary. Glue extended bottom fabric onto box underside, cutting corners as necessary. Cut a piece of fabric ⅛" smaller than box underside. Glue in place to box underside.

❖To cover box inside, cut front, back, and side cardboard pieces and fabric to fit inside box. Spread a thin layer of glue on one side of cardboard pieces. With wrong side up, place inside coordinating fabric onto work surface. Center and glue cardboard pieces onto inside coordinating fabric. Wrap fabric around as before. Glue to inside of box.

❖Glue ½"-wide rose stripe ribbon to base edge of box bottom. Glue narrow cording to bottom edge of stripe ribbon. Glue ¼"-wide velvet ribbon to bottom edge of box top.

•Using Ribbons

❖Refer to General Instructions on pages 19-25.

❖Make three Pansies using ½"-wide grosgrain pale peach ribbon. Cut three 5" lengths.

❖Make one Zigzag Ruched Flower using ⅝"-wide grosgrain peach ribbon.

❖Make two Folded Leaves using ½"-wide stripe rose ribbon. Cut two 9" lengths.

❖Make a small bow using ¼"-wide velvet peach ribbon.

•Finishing

❖Refer to Placement Diagram below. Using hot glue gun and glue stick, hot-glue all ribbon work and bow to front edge of box top.

❖Using industrial-strength glue, attach brass charms to box top at center of side bottom edge. If necessary, slightly bend brass charms to fit over fabric bulk.

Love Letter Box Placement Diagram

Pansy

Zigzag Ruched Flower

Folded Leaf

Soft Blouse

Slippers

Embellished Blazer

Romantic Blouse

Soft Blouse

Materials

Purchased soft blouse

Thread: coordinating

Silk ribbon: 4mm — off-white, 7 yds.

Lace: 7"-wide, 1 yd.; 4"-wide crocheted,
⅝ yd.; 2"-wide delicate, 1⅛ yds.

Trim: tiny picot, 1 yd.

Tools

Needles: chenille (size 20); embroidery
(size 3); hand-sewing

Scissors: fabric

Sewing machine

Directions

•Making Patterns and Cutting Fabrics
❖Refer to General Instructions on pages 8-11.

❖Using fabric scissors, cut 2"-wide lace into two equal lengths.

•Assembling
❖Stitch-straight edge of 2" wide lace to left and right sides of center front placket, tapering lace at bottom edge for a clean finish.

❖Gather 7"-wide lace to fit neck edge, tapering lace at ends to finish. Hand- or machine-stitch to bottom edge of collar band.

❖Hand- or machine-stitch 4"-wide crocheted lace to collar band. Gather lace slightly at bottom of collar band so lace lays flat against bottom edge of collar band. Gather top edge of lace slightly to fit top edge of collar band. Turn lace under at neck edge fronts to finish.

❖Refer to Placement Diagram below. Swirl and hand-stitch tiny picot trim to collar and front placket.

•Embroidery
❖Refer to General Instructions on pages 14-19.

❖Embroider design onto collar and placket front near tiny picot trim, following Ribbon Embroidery Color and Stitch Guide below.

Soft Blouse • Ribbon Embroidery Color and Stitch Guide
Silk ribbons listed below are 4mm unless otherwise indicated.

Step		Ribbon Color	Stitch
1	Assorted Clusters	Off-white	Bullion Lazy Daisy
2	Assorted Clusters	Off-white	Loop Petal Stitch
3	Assorted Clusters	Off-white	Ribbon Stitch

Soft Blouse
Placement Diagram

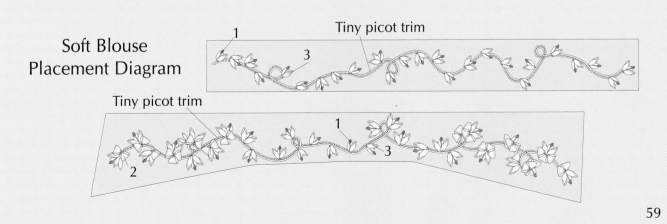

$\mathscr{Slippers}$

Shown on page 58.

Materials

Purchased ivory slippers, suitable for
  embroidery

Silk ribbons: 4mm — ivory, off-white, pale
  peach, pale yellow, 2½ yds. each

Hand-dyed ribbon: 4mm — yellow, 2 yds.

Tools

Needles: chenille (size 20)

Scissors: fabric

Slippers Transfer Sheet Full Size

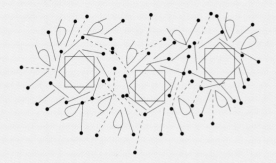

Slippers Placement Diagram

Directions

•Embroidery

❖Refer to General Instructions on pages 14-19.

❖Refer to Transfer Sheet and Placement Diagram.
Embroider design onto slippers following Ribbon
Embroidery Color and Stitch Guide below.

❖To avoid having knots on inside of slippers, hide
ribbon knots within embroidery.

Slippers • Ribbon Embroidery Color and Stitch Guide
Silk ribbons listed below are 4mm unless otherwise indicated.

Step		Ribbon Color	Stitch
1	Rose Centers	Yellow (hand-dyed)	Wool Rose
2	Rose Middle	Pale Peach	Ribbon Stitch, 1-Twist Ribbon Stitch
	✿Stitch Ribbon Stitches around rose centers.		
3	Leaves	Ivory	Bullion Lazy Daisy
4	Petals	Pale Yellow	Ribbon Stitch, 1-Twist Ribbon Stitch
5	Petals	Off-White	Ribbon Stitch, 1-Twist Ribbon Stitch
	✿Stitch off-white petals to fill out roses.		

✿*Additional Stitch Information*

Embellished Blazer

Directions

•Assembling

❖Using straight pins, mark outer lapel edge and collar edge every 2". With hand-sewing needle and coordinating thread, place a ⅜" stitch at marks and gather so edge becomes slightly scalloped.

•Embroidery

❖Refer to General Instructions on pages 14-19.

❖Refer to Placement Diagram on page 62. Embroider design to lapel and collar of blazer following Ribbon Embroidery Color and Stitch Guide below.

❖To make embroidery neat on underside of lapels, stitch ribbon or floss through underside of lapel near beginning point, leaving a ½" ribbon end extended out from lapel. Take a very small back-stitch, then bring ribbon to front lapel surface to begin stitching. Trim extended ribbon flush to lapel underside. End stitching in same manner, securing ribbon end on lapel underside. When moving from one stitch to next, stitch in-between lapel layers.

Shown on page 58.

Materials

Purchased blazer of choice

Thread: coordinating

Silk ribbons: 4mm — blue green, med. blue green, bronze, dk. heather, dusty purple, olive green, dk. olive green, bright rose, deep rose, wine, deep wine, 3 yds. each

Embroidery floss: bronze green

Tools

Needles: chenille (size 20); hand-sewing

Ruler

Scissors: fabric

Straight pins

Embellished Blazer • Ribbon Embroidery Color and Stitch Guide

Silk ribbons listed below are 4mm unless otherwise indicated.
Embroidery floss listed below is three strands unless otherwise indicated.

Step		Ribbon and Floss Color	Stitch
1	Stems	Bronze Green Floss (6 Strands) Whipped with Olive Green	Whipped Running Stitch
2	Stems	Bronze Green Floss (6 Strands) Whipped with Blue Green	Whipped Running Stitch
3	Stems	Bronze Green Floss (6 Strands) Whipped with Bronze	Whipped Running Stitch
4	Flower Center	Bright Rose	Bullion Lazy Daisy, Ribbon Stitch, 1-Twist Ribbon Stitch
5	Flower Center	Wine	Knotted Lazy Daisy
6	Petals	Deep Rose	Ribbon Stitch, 1-Twist Ribbon Stitch, Bullion Lazy Daisy
7	Petals	Deep Wine	Ribbon Stitch, 1-Twist Ribbon Stitch
8	Petals	Dusty Purple	Ribbon Stitch, 1-Twist Ribbon Stitch
9	Petals	Dk. Heather, Deep Rose	Loop Petal Stitch
10	All Leaves	Bronze, Dk. Olive Green, Med. Blue Green, Olive Green, Blue Green	Lazy Daisy Stitch

Embellished Blazer Placement Diagram

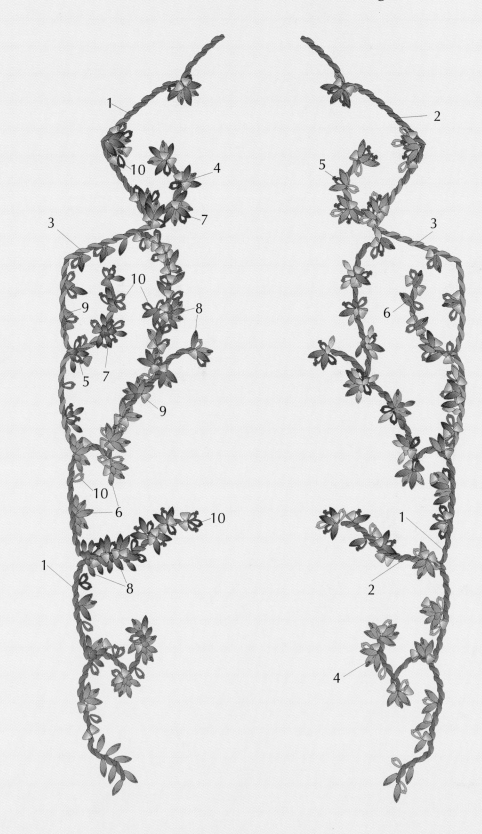

Romantic Blouse

Shown on page 58.

Materials

Blouse pattern of choice: with or without peplum

Fabrics: 45"-wide voile, organza, or batiste, 2-3 yds., for blouse base; linen, or lace, such as a table runner, tea towels, or napkins, for peplum fabric; handkerchief or napkin, to stitch onto blouse base fabric, (4); several large pieces of linen such as 18"-diameter table topper, or old aprons

Thread: coordinating

Assorted ribbon: ⅞"-wide satin double-face, peach, 1 yd.

Lace: 2-3"-wide edging, four lengths, ⅝ yd. (4), for blouse base; lace pieces, small filler type; lace piece, or premade lace collar, for collar fabric

Facing, interfacing, and elastic: as required by pattern

Doilies: 8"-diameter (3), to stitch onto blouse base fabric; 12"-diameter (2), for collar

Appliqués: small (2-3)

Buttons: as needed

Tools

Needles: hand-sewing

Iron and ironing board

Scissors: fabric

Sewing machine

Straight pins

Directions

•Making Patterns and Cutting Fabrics

❖Refer to General Instructions on pages 8-11.

❖Add ¾" seam allowance to blouse pattern. Using fabric scissors, cut out blouse front, back, and sleeves from blouse base fabric. Seam allowance will be trimmed off once linens and laces have been stitched to blouse base fabric. Do not cut out facing, cuffs, or peplum from blouse base fabric.

•Assembling

❖Refer to General Instructions on pages 13-14.

❖To assemble blouse, old linens are stitched onto blouse base fabric. This base fabric relieves any stress that could be placed on linens from washing or wearing.

❖Press each piece of linen and lace. Collage the bodice fronts at neck edge, using the two 12" doilies. See (1) on page 64. Allow 12" doilies to surround entire neck edge. Pin in place. Use remaining doily halves for back neck edge. See (2) on page 64.

❖Position and pin lace edgings at center front overlap. If pattern has attached facing extending from center front, trim extension off, leaving a ⅝" seam allowance. Seam a piece of facing fabric when assembling blouse rather than wasting linens or lace. See (3) on page 64. Place all other linens and appliqués on blouse front. When satisfied, stitch in place. See (4) on page 64. Press frequently while stitching linens in place.

❖Repeat process for back and sleeves.

❖Replace pattern pieces over lace collaged front, back, and sleeves. Recut collaged pieces on cutting lines. Mark appropriately.

❖If applicable, cut peplum from peplum fabric. Allow for front facings to be cut from facing fabric. Assemble blouse following pattern instructions. Use interfacing, if necessary, for stability.

•Finishing

❖Finish neck edge with special collar. Use finished edge of handkerchief or napkin for cuffs. Complete blouse with finishing touches such as buttonholes and buttons.

❖Make a peach satin bow for front at neck closure.

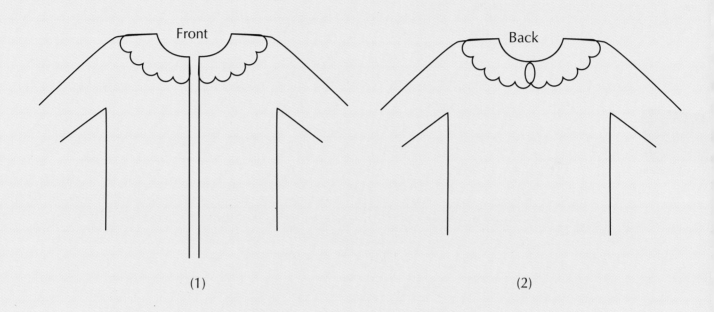

(1)

(2)

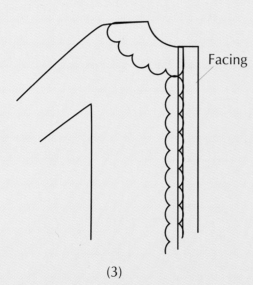

Facing

(3)

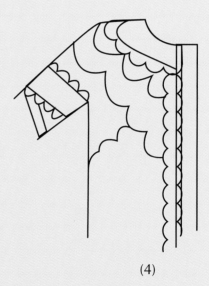

(4)

Stationery Folder

Shown on page 65.

Materials

Fabrics: jacquard, ecru, ⅓ yd.; floral, ecru, ½ yd.

Thread: coordinating

Assorted ribbons: ½"-wide grosgrain, ecru, 2 yds.; cafe, ½ yd.; pale green, ¼ yd.

Lace: ivory, 12" x 12", with scalloped edge

Trim: ⅜"-wide tatted, ½ yd.

Quilt batting: 11" x 19"

Doily: 4" tatted, dyed shell pink

Double-sided fusible web: 1⅜ yds.

Cardboard: lightweight, 1 sheet; heavy, 10" x 32"

Tools

Brown paper bag

Glue: craft, thin-bodied; hot glue gun and glue sticks

Marking tool

Iron and ironing board

Needles: hand-sewing

Ruler

Scissors: craft; fabric

Straight pins

Wet and dry rags

Directions

•Making Patterns and Cutting Fabrics

❖Refer to General Instructions on pages 8-11.

❖Refer to Stationery Folder Patterns on page 69.

Using craft scissors, cut one heavy cardboard for front flap pattern, and one each for back and front 9½" x 7". Cut one lightweight cardboard for front flap liner pattern, one inside front liner 9⅜" x 6¾", one inside back liner 9⅜" x 6¾", one pocket front section pattern, one pocket middle section pattern, and one pocket back section 9¼" x 6¾".

❖Add ¾" seam allowance. Using fabric scissors cut one floral fabric for front flap liner pattern, one pocket front section pattern, one pocket middle section pattern, one inside front liner 9⅜" x 6¾", one inside back liner 9⅜" x 6¾", and one back pocket section 9¼" x 6¾". Cut one jacquard fabric for front flap pattern, and one each for back and front 9½" x 7". Cut one lace for front flap pattern.

❖No seam allowance necessary. Cut one floral fabric for rear pocket strip 47" x 2", and two pocket side strips 3" x 14". Cut one jacquard fabric for top binding strip 20" x 2⅝", and one bottom binding strip 20" x 2". Cut one fusible web for top binding strip 9½" x 2⅝", one bottom binding strip 9½" x 2", and one rear pocket strip 23½" x 2". Cut one left, and one right fusible web for pocket side pattern.

❖Place and label fabric cuts with corresponding cardboard pieces.

•Assembling

❖Refer to General Instructions on pages 11-12.

❖Pad front flap, back, and front cardboard with batting. Trim batting flush to cardboard's edge and bevel inward slightly.

❖Using hot glue gun and glue stick, snugly wrap and hot-glue front flap, back, and front with jacquard fabric. Eliminate bulk at corners. Wrap lace around front flap.

❖Laminate front flap liner, inside back liner, inside front liner, back pocket section, and middle pocket section. Trim all bulk from corners and clip curves.

❖For front pocket section, laminate two short edges and top curved edge with corresponding fabric. Leave fabric unwrapped at bottom edge. This will be used later as a tab.

❖Press under short ends of top binding strip ½". Apply double-sided fusible web to middle of top binding strip, following manufacturer's instructions. See (1). Peel off fusible web backing. Fold ends of strip over to meet at center. See (2). Fuse in place.

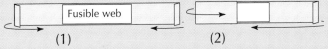

(1)   (2)

❖Hot-glue raw edge of fused top binding strip to underside edge of front flap; overlap strip ½" onto straight edge of front flap. See (3).

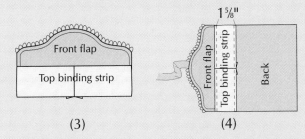

(3)   (4)

❖Finger-gather tatted trim to underside bottom edge of front flap. Cut 12" from grosgrain ribbon. Hot-glue edge of grosgrain ribbon to underside of front flap liner at center for front tie. With wrong sides together, hot-glue front flap liner to front flap.

❖Measure and mark 1⅝" from edge of front flap onto top binding strip. Hot-glue remaining raw edge of fused top binding strip to underside edge of back on mark. See (4).

❖To assemble rear pocket and front pocket sections, press under short ends of rear pocket strip ½". See (1) on page 66. Apply fusible web to middle of strip. Peel off fusible web backing. Fold ends of strip over to meet at center. Fuse in place. See (2) on page 66.

❖Press strip in half, matching raw edges. Measure strip to mark center. See (5).

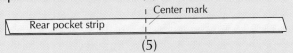

(5)

❖Mark center of one long edge of inside back liner. Place inside back liner on work surface. Match center mark of rear pocket strip to center mark of inside back liner, having creased edge inward. See (6). Hot-glue strip onto marked edge of inside back liner with ½" allowance.

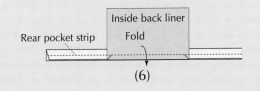

(6)

❖At corners, diagonally cut strip to enable strip to turn the corner. Hot-glue strip onto short edge of inside back liner with ½" allowance. See (7). Repeat with remaining edge. Set aside.

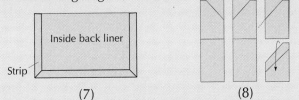

(7)   (8)

❖Fold and crease pocket side fabric strip in half, matching short edges. Fuse left and right pocket sides to each strip. See (8). Peel off fusible web backing. Fold strip up onto fusible web and fuse in place. Trim excess from top edge. Diagonally trim remaining edge to 1". Fuse strip of fusible web onto excess at top edge. Peel off fusible web backing and fuse in place for a clean edge finish to front pocket sides.

❖Press front left and right pocket sides, accordion style. See (9).

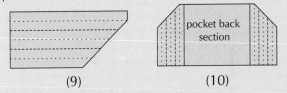

(9)   (10)

❖With wrong side up, place pocket back section on work surface. Hot-glue long edge of front pocket sides to wrong side of one short edge of pocket back section. Hot-glue long edge of remaining front pocket side to wrong side of remaining short edge of pocket back section. See (10). Turn right side up.

❖With wrong side up, hot-glue 1" tab from pocket front section to right side of pocket back section at bottom edge. See (11).

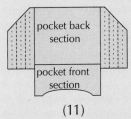

(11)

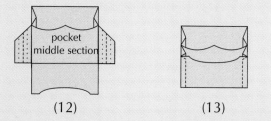

(12)

(13)

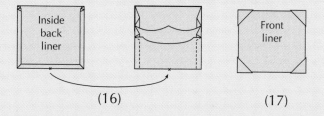

(16)

(17)

❖Fold pocket sides over onto pocket back section and repress. Hot-glue middle accordion pleat of pocket side to underside of one short edge of pocket middle section, with pocket middle section right side up. Hot-glue opposite middle accordion pleats of pocket side to underside of remaining short edge of pocket middle section. See (12) on page 67.

❖Press pocket sides again into accordion pleat to reinforce shape. Fold up pocket section onto pleated front pocket sides. Hot-glue shortest edge of pocket sides to underside short edges of pocket front section. See (13).

❖Press under short ends of bottom binding strip ½". See (1) on page 66. Apply fusible web to middle of strip. Peel off fusible web backing. Fold ends of strip over to meet at center. See (2) on page 66. Fuse in place.

❖Hot-glue raw edge of fused bottom binding strip to underside bottom edge of pocket back section; overlap strip ½" onto bottom edge of pocket back section. See (14).

❖With wrong side up, measure 1" from edge of pocket back section onto bottom binding strip. Hot-glue remaining raw edge of fused bottom binding strip to edge of front on wrong side; overlap strip ½" onto bottom edge of front. See (15).

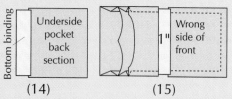

(14)

(15)

❖Mark center of bottom underside edge of pocket back section. Match center mark of remaining raw edge of rear pocket strip to center mark of pocket back section. Hot-glue strip onto underside of marked edge of pocket back section with ½" allowance. (Note: Hot-glue small sections at a time

and make certain hot-glue is thoroughly flattened before proceeding.) See (16).

❖At corners, diagonally cut strip to enable strip to turn corner. Hot-glue strip onto short edges of pocket back section with ½" allowance.

❖Cut one 3" x 18" strip of floral fabric. Press strip in half, matching long edges. Cut four equal sections. Wrap and hot-glue corners of front liner with pressed sections, creating corner pockets. Trim all bulk from underside. See (17). With wrong sides together, hot-glue front liner to front. Hot-glue inside back liner to back.

❖Hand-stitch scalloped edge of lace to top edge of front flap. Trim lace at sides and turn under ¾". Extend lace over top binding and onto back. Turn lace diagonally under, forming a point at bottom. See (18). Pin in place. Cut 20" from grosgrain ribbon. Stitch end under lace point. Hand-stitch lace in place.

(18)

•Using Ribbons

❖Refer to General Instructions on pages 19-25.

❖Make two ecru and one cafe Rosettes from remaining grosgrain ribbon. Cut 18" length for each rosette.

❖Make three Folded Leaves from pale green grosgrain ribbon. Cut three 3" lengths.

•Finishing

❖Refer to Placement Diagram on page 69.

❖Gather-stitch 4" doily down to 2" so doily ruffles slightly. Hot-glue to center bottom edge of front flap.

❖Hot-glue folded leaves and rosettes to doily ruffle.

Stationery Folder Patterns
Enlarge 280%

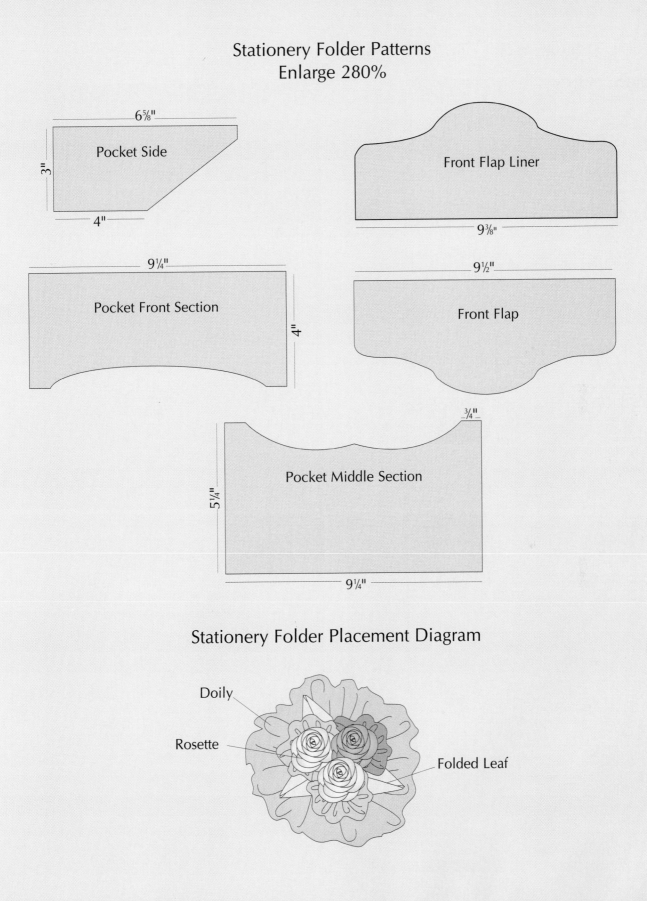

Pocket Side
6⅝"
3"
4"

Front Flap Liner
9⅜"

Pocket Front Section
9¼"
4"

Front Flap
9½"

Pocket Middle Section
¾"
5¼"
9¼"

Stationery Folder Placement Diagram

Doily

Rosette

Folded Leaf

Hand Towel

Jewelry Box

Lady Pincushion

Ribbon Work Frame

Hand Towel

Materials

Fabric: linen, 14" x 17"

Thread: coordinating

Silk ribbons: 4mm — blush, ¾ yd.; gray-green, rose, dk. rose, ⅜ yd. each

Assorted ribbon: ⅝"-wide satin, pale peach, ½ yd.

Lace: ¼"-wide insertion, ⅜"-wide scalloped, 1½ yds.; 1½"-wide galloon, 3"-wide Venice, ½ yd. each; lace rosette

Tools

Scissors: fabric

Sewing machine

Directions

•Assembling

❖Use very narrow stitch for all zigzag stitching.

❖Narrowly hem one 14" cut edge of linen. Match straight edge of 3"-wide lace up to hemmed edge. Zigzag-stitch edges together.

❖Match edge of satin ribbon up to straight edge of 3"-wide lace. Zigzag-stitch edges together over linen.

❖Thread 4mm blush ribbon through insertion lace. Zigzag-stitch insertion lace over joined edges of Venice lace and satin ribbon.

❖Overlap galloon lace over satin ribbon and stitch in place onto linen fabric.

❖Narrowly hem towel at sides and top. Zigzag-stitch ⅜"-wide scalloped lace over seam to finish.

•Using Ribbons

❖Make small bow using remaining 4mm ribbons. Knot ends.

•Finishing

❖Stitch knot of bow to center of towel at ribbon row. Stitch lace rosette over bow knot. Fold towel in thirds.

Jewelry Box

Materials

Fabrics: inside lid fabric, 10" x 12"; back drop fabric, 10" x 12"; 1½"-wide strips, sheer or lightweight, coral, ivory, pale green, peach, for flowers; felt, 10" x 12"

Thread: coordinating

Lace: ½"-wide, ⅜ yd. each (4); ½"-wide lace for dahlia ruffle, 1¼"-wide crocheted, ¼ yd. each; 2"-wide beaded lace

Trim: ½"-wide gold metallic, 2 yds.; tiny picot, 1 yd.; chenille, olive green, ¾ yd.

Cardboard: lightweight, 8" x 10"

Quilt batting: 8" x 10"

Charms: brass filigree fans, small (3); brass floral (2)

Buttons: mother-of-pearl, small (15); center button

Beads: pearl, small (3)

Leaves: lavender, small (2)

Decorative paper: 8" x 10"

Florist tape: to wrap coral sprays

Paint: of choice

Wire: lightweight, green cotton-covered, ½ yd.

Screws: small (3)

Hinges: small (2)

Continued on page 72

Continued from page 71

Slide hinge

Brads: small (8-10)

Shadow box: 8" x 10"

Picture frame: 8" x 10"

Tools

Glue: craft; hot glue gun and glue sticks; industrial-strength

Needles: hand-sewing

Paintbrush

Scissors: craft; fabric

Screwdriver

Directions

•Assembling

❖Using paint of choice and paintbrush, paint shadow box and picture frame. Let paint dry thoroughly.

❖To make jewelry box, back side of shadow box becomes inside top of jewelry box.

❖Remove cardboard from back side of shadow box and glass from front of shadow box.

❖Replace cardboard in shadow box for bottom. Cut and place decorative paper, right side up, on top of cardboard. Place glass on top of decorative paper.

❖Cut felt to cover bottom of shadow box. Using craft glue, attach to edge of shadow box. This will hold glass, cardboard, and decorative paper inside shadow box bottom.

❖Pad cardboard for picture frame with batting. Trim batting flush to cardboard's edge and bevel inward slightly. Wrap with front fabric. Trim bulk from corners.

•Using Fabrics as Ribbons

❖Refer to General Instructions on pages 19-25.

❖Rather than ribbon, pressed fabric strips with a finished edge are used. Techniques are used identical to those of ribbon work, which shows that any ribbon work technique can be modified to create flowers from fabrics. When creating ribbon work from fabric, it is best to use delicate, lightweight, or sheer fabrics such as organza, chiffon, charmuese, crepe de chine, organdy, and china silk. A minute amount of fabric is needed for flowers. Make use of scraps.

❖Assemble flower work from fabric following Flower Work, Embellishment, and Instruction Guide on page 73.

•Finishing

❖Refer to Transfer Sheet and Placement Diagram on page 74. Using hot glue gun and glue stick, arrange and hot-glue flower work onto backdrop fabric.

❖Using industrial-strength glue, attach brass charms, buttons, and beads.

❖Glue 2"-wide beaded lace in place.

❖Hot-glue three coral sprays in place.

❖Hot-glue single petal rose, gathered rose, and dahlia in place, covering stems of two coral sprays.

❖Hot-glue three peach blossoms in place, covering stem of one coral spray with one peach blossom. Glue pearl beads in center of each peach blossom.

❖Gather bottom edge of crocheted lace; taper thread at both ends, creating a fan. Hot-glue in place underneath dahlia.

❖Hot-glue all leaves in place. Hide ends under flowers.❖Slightly bend three brass filigree fans. Glue in place under single petal rose and gathered rose.

❖Glue two brass floral pieces under dahlia.

❖Drape and tack tiny picot trim in place.

❖Make a six-looped bow using chenille trim. Hot-glue in place under dahlia. Drape bow ends.

❖Hot-glue ½"-wide laces to outer cardboard edges.

❖Glue small mother-of-pearl buttons in place.

❖Place flower work in frame. Wrap second piece of cardboard with inside lid fabric. Trim bulk from corners. With wrong sides together, place inside box cardboard in back of flower work.

❖Place flower work frame on top of shadow box. Use brads to hold cardboard in place. Attach hinges at back. Attach slide hinge to inside right corner.

❖Glue ½"-wide gold metallic trim to underside of flower work frame to hide brads. Glue ½"-wide gold metallic trim to edge of glass inside shadow box.

Jewelry Box • Flower Work, Embellishment, and Instruction Guide

Step		Fabric Color	Flower Stitch
1	Flower Spray	1½"-Wide Sheer Coral Fabric	Gathered Rosebud

❂Press 39" strip of fabric in half, matching raw edges. Cut fabric into thirteen 3" lengths. Make a total of thirteen gathered rosebuds. For coral spray, fold a 6" length of lightweight wire in half. Stitch or glue five of the gathered rosebuds onto wire, spacing gathered rosebuds so they are ¼" apart. Wrap wire with florist tape to hide raw edges. Repeat for a second spray of five gathered rosebuds and a third spray of three gathered rosebuds.

2	Flower	1½"-Wide Ivory Fabric	Dahlia, Single Fold
		½"-Wide Lace	
		1"-Wide Pale Peach Fabric	

❂Press 27" strip ivory fabric in half, matching raw edges. Cut thirteen 2" lengths. Make one single fold dahlia. For lace ruffle for center of dahlia, fold 5" piece of ½"-wide lace in half, matching raw edges. Stitch or glue narrow seam. Gather-stitch along bottom edge. Pull gathers and secure thread. Glue lace ruffle to center of dahlia. For pale peach ruffle above lace ruffle, cut 1"-wide piece of pale peach fabric into one 7" length. Press in half, matching raw edges. Fold in half, matching short raw edges. Stitch or glue narrow seam. Gather-stitch along bottom edges ¼" up from raw edges. Pull gathers tight and secure thread. Trim raw edges to ⅛" below stitching. Glue pale peach ruffle to center of dahlia above lace ruffle. Glue center button to center of dahlia.

3	Flower	1½"-Wide Pale Green Fabric	Single Petal Rose

❂Press 22" strip of fabric in thirds, creating two finished edges, so fabric measures about ¾" wide when pressed. Make one single petal rose.

4	Flower	1½"-Wide Peach Fabric	Gathered Rosebud

❂Press 15" strip fabric in half, matching raw edges. Make one gathered rosebud.

5	Leaves	1½"-Wide Pale Green Fabric	Folded Leaf

❂Press 15" strip fabric in half, matching raw edges. Cut fabric into five 3" lengths. Make five folded leaves.

6	Flowers	1½"-Wide Sheer Peach Fabric	Peach Blossom

❂Press 25" length of fabric in half, matching raw edges. Make three peach blossoms.

❂*Additional Stitch Information*

Jewelry Box Transfer Sheet
Enlarge 165%

Jewelry Box
Placement Diagram

1

3

4

2" beaded la

6

2

5

Lady Pincushion

Shown on page 70.

Materials

Fabrics: brocade, pale gold, ¼ yd.; chiffon, pale gold, ⅜ yd.

Thread: coordinating

Silk ribbons: 4mm — lt. blue, 1 yd.; dk. rose, ¼ yd.; 7mm — lt. rose, ¼ yd.; med. rose ¼ yd.; 1¼"-wide ivory, ½ yd.

Assorted ribbons: ¼"-wide sheer, gold, ¼ yd.; 1½"-wide velvet, chartreuse, ¼ yd.; ⅝"-wide wired, rose, ¼ yd.

Lace: ¾"-wide French Valenciennes, 1 yd.; 2½"-wide ivory, ½ yd.

Stuffing: polyester

Cardboard: heavy, 6" x 16"

Pipe cleaner: white

Craft sticks: (2)

Porcelain doll head with shoulder plates

Tools

Iron and ironing board

Needles: hand-sewing

Glue: hot glue gun and glue sticks

Marking tool

Ruler

Scissors: craft; fabric

Sewing machine

Wire cutters

Directions

•Making Patterns and Cutting Fabrics

❖Refer to General Instructions on pages 8-11.

❖See Oval Pattern below. Using craft scissors, cut four ovals from cardboard. Layer and hot-glue three ovals together. Set aside.

❖Using fabric scissors, cut a 3" x 4" piece of pale gold brocade fabric for bodice.

•Assembling

❖Fold pale gold brocade fabric in half, matching the 3" cut edges. Stitch ¼" seam. See (1). Finger-press seam open. Place seam at center back of tube. Stitch end edge. See (2).

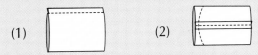

(1)   (2)

❖Using hot glue gun and glue stick, layer and hot-glue two craft sticks together. Hot-glue top edge of craft sticks to top seamed edge of bodice. See (3). Turn bodice right side out so craft sticks are inside. Using polyester stuffing, stuff bodice. Baste-stitch open edge closed, while nipping in at waist to cinch. See (4). Hot-glue curved edge of fabric to inside of porcelain shoulders.

(3)   (4)

❖See Sleeve Pattern below. Cut two enlarged pieces of pale gold brocade fabric for sleeves. Fold one piece in half, matching tapered edges. Stitch ¼" seam, turning up bottom edge ¼" to finish. See (5). Place seam at center back of tapered tube, as done for bodice. Stitch wide end of tapered tube closed. See (6). Using wire cutters, cut pipe cleaner in half. Curl up one end of pipe cleaner. Hot-glue curl to top seamed edge of sleeve. See (7). Turn right side out. Using polyester stuffing, stuff lightly to shape, leaving pipe cleaner extended out of sleeve.

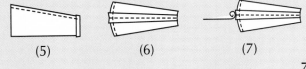

(5)   (6)   (7)

Lady Pincushion Patterns
Enlarge 280%

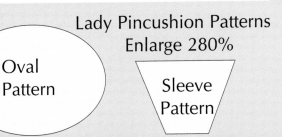

Oval Pattern

Sleeve Pattern

❖Repeat for other sleeve. Hot-glue top finished edge of each sleeve to side of bodice at shoulders. Let hot glue dry thoroughly. Twist pipe cleaners together at "hands" so arms are in front of bodice. Using wire cutters, trim excess pipe cleaners off just past twisting. Bouquet will be hot-glued over twisted area later.

❖For gown underskirt, cut a 15" x 5½" piece of pale gold brocade fabric. Fold fabric in half, matching short edges. Stitch ¼" seam at short edges. Press seam open. Turn right side out.

❖Hot-glue one spot on bottom edge of gown to underside edge of single layered cardboard oval at center of one long oval side. At opposite edge of cardboard oval, hot-glue opposite edge of gown to bottom underside edge of cardboard oval. Continue to hot-glue bottom gown to cardboard oval, creating a cup of fabric with cardboard base. Turn fabric, cup side up. Using polyester stuffing, firmly stuff gown fabric. Turn under top edge of gown, then gather-stitch along folded edge.

❖Create small hole in center of polyester stuffing. Place craft sticks into hole. Tightly pull gather stitch to close around bodice and secure thread.

❖For gown overskirt, cut pale gold chiffon fabric 8" x 44". Fold back each short edge about 2" and pin to hold. Fold down one long edge of chiffon fabric about ½" and machine gather-stitch as close to fold as possible. Stitch second row of machine gather-stitches ⅛" away from first row. Repeat for remaining long edge. It is not necessary to fold under this edge before stitching. Pull gather stitching on folded down edge so fabric fits waist and turned-back edges meet at center front. Secure to gown underskirt at waist.

❖Pull gather stitches along remaining long edge to fit bottom oval cardboard. Hot-glue raw edge to underside of cardboard. Chiffon fabric will float over underskirt.

❖Cut piece of pale gold brocade fabric ¾" larger than cardboard oval shape. Tightly wrap and hot-glue pale gold brocade fabric around 3-layered oval cardboards. With wrong sides together, hot-glue wrapped cardboard oval to underskirt oval.

❖Wrap 1½"-wide chartreuse velvet ribbon tightly around bodice. Secure ribbon at center back.

❖Gather-stitch 2½"-wide lace ⅝" down from top finished edge and taper gather stitches. Pull gathers to fit shoulders. Hot-glue or sew in place. Cut 18" from ¾"-wide French Valenciennes lace. Gather-stitch along top edge. Pull gathers to fit shoulders and place second ruffle under shoulder ruffle. Stitch again 1⅛" away from first gather stitch row on 2½"-wide lace. Pull gathers to fit shoulders so a doubled, folded ruffle is formed. Secure gather stitches.

•Using Ribbons

❖Refer to General Instructions on pages 19-25.

❖Make one Zigzag Ruched Flower, by using ⅝"-wide wired rose ribbon. Mark ¾" intervals for a total of eleven intervals on one edge and ten intervals on other edge. Gather-stitch. Pull gathers so ribbon measures 2⅛". Join first to last petal having edge with ten petals facing inward. Stitch center of first inward petal to center of second inward petal. Continue to join all inward petals at center. Twist and place raw edges of ribbon on underside of flower.

❖Make one Gathered Rosebud by layering both shades of 7mm ribbon and 4mm dk. rose ribbon, holding all three ribbons together as one.

❖Make a small bow, length desired, using 4mm lt. blue ribbon. Make a slightly larger bow, length desired, using ¼"-wide sheer gold ribbon.

•Finishing

❖Hot-glue gathered rosebud to center of zigzag ruched flower to make bouquet. Center bouquet over twisted pipe cleaners and hot-glue.

❖Hot-glue gold bow to center front bodice at shoulder edge. Hot-glue lt. blue bow to center of gold bow.

❖Gather-stitch remaining ¾"-wide lace along top edge. Tightly gather to fit waist. Hot-glue or sew lace ruffle to waist.

❖Make a bow, length desired, using 1¼"-wide ivory ribbon. Fork-cut ribbon tails. See (8). Hot-glue knot of bow to center back of bodice at waist. Make a small bow, length desired, with 4mm lt. blue ribbon and hot-glue on top of ivory bow.

(8)

Ribbon Work Frame

Shown on page 70.
Materials

Fabric: background, 14" square

Thread: coordinating

For Dahlia

Assorted ribbons: 1¼"-wide woven, ivory, 1½ yds.; 1"-wide ombre, pale yellow/lt. green, 1 yd.

Bead: silver, large

For Half Zinnia

Silk ribbon: 4mm — pale peach, 1⅛ yds., for stamens

Assorted ribbon: 1"-wide ombre, pale mauve/peach, 1⅛ yds.

For Daisy

Assorted ribbon: ¼"-wide velvet, peach; ⅛"-wide velvet, tan, 1¼ yds. each

Buttons: small mother-of-pearl (3), for center

Cameo: small

For Fuchsia

Assorted ribbon: 2"-wide cross-dyed, coral, ⅜ yd.

Embroidery floss: green, for stems

Stamens: small (12) *For Pansy*

Assorted ribbon: ½"-wide grosgrain, dusty purple, ½ yd.

Rhinestones: small (3), for center

For Leaves

Assorted ribbons: ⅝"-wide satin, pale olive green, ⅝ yd.; 1"-wide ombre, lt. green/brown, ¼ yd.

For Bow

Silk ribbons: 4mm — blush, dusty purple, lt. orchid, ¾ yd. each

Frame: of choice, 8" x 10"

Tools

Iron and ironing board

Needles: hand-sewing; milliner's

Glue: hot glue gun and glue sticks; industrial-strength

Ruler

Scissors: fabric

Directions

•Using Ribbons

❖Refer to General Instructions on pages 19-25.

❖Refer to Transfer Sheet and Placement Diagram on page 79. Assemble all ribbon work flowers following Flower Work, Embellishment, and Instruction Guide on page 78.

•Finishing

❖Using hot glue gun and glue stick, arrange and hot-glue flower work onto background fabric.

❖Using industrial-strength glue, attach bead, buttons, cameo, and rhinestones. Stitch or glue four stamens into center of each fuchsia.

❖Glue large silver bead to center of dahlia. Glue three small mother-of-pearl buttons to center of peach velvet daisy. Glue small cameo to center of tan velvet daisy. Glue three small rhinestones to center of pansies.

❖Place in frame of choice and secure.

Ribbon Work Frame • Flower Work, Embellishment, and Instruction Guide

Silk ribbons listed below are 4mm unless otherwise indicated.
Embroidery floss listed below is three strands unless otherwise indicated.

Step		Ribbon and Floss Color	Flower Stitch
1	Flower, Outer	1¼"-Wide Woven Ivory	Dahlia, Double Fold
	✪Cut seventeen 3" lengths. Make one double fold dahlia.		
2	Flower, Center	1"-Wide Ombre Pale Yellow/Lt. Green	Dahlia, Double Fold
	✪Cut thirteen 2½" lengths. Make one double fold dahlia. Place pale yellow edge of ribbon at top so it will be outer edge of each petal. Stitch or hot-glue pale yellow/lt. green petal dahlia to middle of ivory petal dahlia.		
3	Flower Petals	1"-Wide Ombre Pale Mauve/Peach	Half Zinnia
	✪Cut thirteen petals. Make one half zinnia.		
4	Flower	¼"-Wide Velvet Peach	Daisy
	✪Cut twenty 2⅛" lengths. Make one daisy.		
5	Flower	⅛"-Wide Velvet Tan	Daisy
	✪Cut twenty-one 2⅛" lengths. Chain gather-stitch twelve petals together. Gather and secure thread. Chain gather-stitch nine petals together. Gather and secure thread. Do not join last petal to first. Stitch or glue 9-petal layer over 12-petal layer, positioning outer edge of 9-petal layer slightly down from outer edge of 12-petal layer.		
6	Flower	2"-Wide Cross-dyed Coral, Green Floss	Fuchsia
	✪Cut three 4" lengths. Make three fuchsias. Use 6" length of green floss (6 strand)s for each fuchsia stem.		
7	Flower	½"-Wide Grosgrain Dusty Purple	Pansy
	✪Cut three 5" lengths. Make three pansies.		
8	Leaf	⅝"-Wide Satin Pale Olive Green	Gathered Leaf
	✪Cut five 4" lengths. Make five gathered leaves.		
9	Leaf	1"-Wide Ombre Lt. Green/Brown	Folded Leaf
	✪Cut three 3" lengths. Make three folded leaves.		
10	Bow	Blush, Dusty Purple, Lt. Orchid	Cascade Stitch
	✪Make one small bow. Stitch knot of bow under bottom right corner of half zinnia. Cascade stitch ribbon ends.		
11	Stamens	Pale Peach	Knotted Mum
	✪Cut fifteen 2½" lengths. Make one knotted mum. Stitch or hot-glue to center of half zinnia for stamens.		

✪*Additional Stitch Information*

Ribbon Work Frame Transfer Sheet
Enlarge 200%

Ribbon Work Frame
Placement Diagram

Silk Camisole

Tank Top

Wreath

Window Garland

80

Silk Camisole

Materials

Purchased silk camisole, lace-edged

Silk ribbons: 4mm — blush, 5 yds.; lt. coral, 3 yds.; pale green, 2 yds.; pale olive, pale orchid, 1½ yds. each; peach, 4 yds.; pale pink, 3½ yds.; 7mm — apricot, 1½ yds.

Tools

Needles: chenille (size 20)

Scissors: fabric

Silk Camisole Placement Diagram

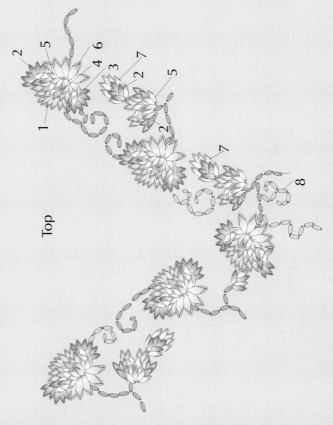

Directions

•Embroidery

❖Refer to General Instructions on pages 14-19.

❖Refer to Placement Diagram. Embroider design onto lace at top edge of camisole following Ribbon Embroidery Color and Stitch Guide below.

❖Keep knotted ends hidden beneath embroidered sections. Do not drag ribbon to next embroidery location. All embroidery done with ribbon stitch is used in a fill-in fashion.

Silk Camisole • Ribbon Embroidery Color and Stitch Guide
Silk ribbons listed below are 4mm unless otherwise indicated.

Step		Ribbon Color	Stitch
1	Flowers, Outer Edges	Peach	Ribbon Stitch
2	Outer Petals, Leaves, Centers	Blush	Ribbon Stitch
3	Middle Petals	Pale Pink	Ribbon Stitch
4	Center Petals	Pale Orchid	Ribbon Stitch, Lazy Daisy
5	Petals, Bottom Edges	Lt. Coral	Ribbon Stitch
6	Flowers, Bottom	Apricot, 7mm	Ribbon Stitch
7	Leaves, Outer Edges	Pale Green	Ribbon Stitch
8	Stems	Pale Olive, Pale Green	Running Stitch
	✿Weave both shades of green through lace as stems.		

✿Additional Stitch Information

Tank Top

Shown on page 80.

Materials

Purchased silk tank top or fabric and pattern to make tank top

Thread: coordinating

Silk ribbons: 4mm — ivory, ¾ yd.; pale peach, 2 yds.

Embroidery floss: silk or rayon, ecru, ivory, pale green, pale peach

Lace: ⅜"-wide, delicate, 1 yd.

Old-fashioned fabric napkin

Tools

Needles: chenille (size 20); hand-sewing; milliner's

Marking tool

Scissors: fabric

Sewing machine

Directions

•Making Patterns and Cutting Fabrics

❖Cut tank top from fabric according to purchased pattern instructions, if applicable.

•Assembling

❖Drape an old-fashioned fabric napkin corner over tank top front. When pleased with placement, mark napkin at neck, shoulder, and armhole locations on wrong side on napkin. Cut napkin ⅝" larger than marked lines. Baste napkin ½" from cut edges so napkin will not stretch out of shape.

•Embroidery

❖Refer to General Instructions on pages 14-19.

❖Refer to Placement Diagram. Embroider design onto napkin edge following Ribbon Embroidery Color and Stitch Guide on page 83.

•Finishing

❖Place embroidered napkin at neck, shoulder, and armhole locations on tank top front. Stitch tank top according to pattern instructions, or place embroidered napkin onto purchased tank top front. Baste-stitch in place. Trim seam allowance to ¼". Turn under on marked lines at neck edge, shoulder seam, and armholes. Hand-stitch in place.

❖Stitch ⅜"-wide lace trim around neck edge front for delicate finish.

Tank Top Placement Diagram

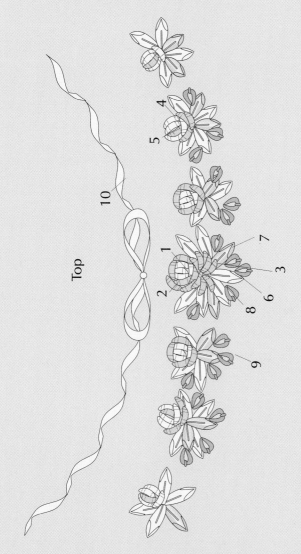

Tank Top • Ribbon Embroidery Color and Stitch Guide

Silk ribbons listed below are 4mm unless otherwise indicated.
Embroidery floss listed below is three strands unless otherwise indicated.

Step		Ribbon and Floss Color	Stitch
1	Centers	Ivory Floss	Bullion Stitch (9 wraps)
2	Petals	Ecru Floss	Bullion Stitch (11 wraps)
	✿Place stitches around ivory Bullion Stitches as petals around three center roses.		
3	Petals	Pale Peach Floss	Bullion Stitch (11 wraps)
	✿Place stitches as larger petals around center rose. Place stitches around ivory center for two roses.		
4	Petals	Ivory Floss	Bullion Stitch (11 wraps)
5	Centers	Pale Peach Floss	Bullion Stitch (7 wraps)
	✿Place at center of four roses.		
6	Petals	Ivory	Ribbon Stitch
	✿Stitch around all roses for color detail.		
7	Petals	Pale Peach	Ribbon Stitch
	✿Stitch around all roses for color detail.		
8	Petal Highlights	Ivory Floss	Straight Stitch
	✿Stitch down center of each ribbon stitch.		
9	Leaves	Pale Green Floss	Lazy Daisy
10	Bow Tails	Pale Peach	Cascade Stitch
	✿Cut 18" length for bow. Secure knot of bow to center front neck edge. Cascade Stitch bow tails.		

✿*Additional Stitch Information*

Wreath

Shown on page 80.

Materials

Fabric: broadcloth, olive green, ¼ yd.

Thread: coordinating

Assorted ribbon: 1½"-wide sheer, mauve,
    2¼ yds.

Cording: ¼"-wide cotton, 2½ yds.

Hat veiling: 2¼ yds.

Doilies: ecru, 2½"-diameter (6); 3"-diameter
    (4); 4"-diameter (3); 6"-diameter (2)

Porcelain doll head with shoulder plate:
    small

Old glove

Cardboard: heavy, 15" x 30"

Old costume jewelry

Greenery: cloth, velvet, or silk flowers (8-9)

Leaves: velvet or satin (2-3 sprays)

Bead spray

Tools

Glue: hot glue gun and glue sticks;
    industrial-strength

Marking tool

Needles: hand-sewing

Scissors: craft; fabric

Straight pins

Directions

•Making Patterns and Cutting Fabrics

❖Refer to General Instructions on pages 8-11.

❖Using marking tool and craft scissors, trace and cut out two 14" circles from cardboard. Trace and cut out 13½" circle in each 14" circle. Hot-glue the two wreath "stabilizers" together. See (1).

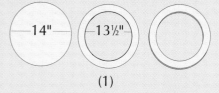

(1)

❖Cut five 1½"-wide strips across width of olive green fabric. Press down one long edge ¼" on each fabric strip.

•Assembling

❖Diagonally wrap wreath stabilizer with fabric strips; overlap finished edges over unfinished edges while wrapping. See (2). Begin and end wrapping on same side of cardboard. This is the underside of wreath. Set aside remaining fabric strips for later use.

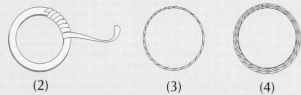

(2)   (3)   (4)

❖Cut one length of cotton cording to equal circumference of cardboard wreath. Hot-glue ends of cording together to form a circle. See (3). Hot-glue a second layer of cording right next to inside edge of first cording circle. See (4). Hot-glue a third layer of cording next to outside edge of first cording circle. See (5). Hot-glue two more layers of cording on top of three-rowed wreath. See (6).

❖Diagonally wrap cording wreath with fabric strips; overlap finished edges over unfinished edges while wrapping. See (7). Begin and end wrapping on underside. Top of wreath is side with two layers of cording.

❖Using industrial-strength glue, attach porcelain doll head's shoulder plate over cording wreath. See (8). Let glue dry thoroughly.

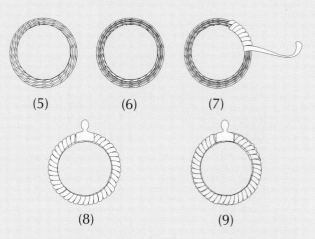

(5)   (6)   (7)

(8)   (9)

❖Glue three 2½", two 4", and four 3" doilies over edges of shoulder plate covering all edges. Gather center of doilies when gluing to shoulder plate.

❖Gather-stitch old glove near wrist area. Secure thread. Arrange and pin glove, flowers, and bead spray around wreath. Use extra leaf sprays and doilies as fillers between flowers. Once flowers are placed, stitch or hot-glue them to cording wreath. Fold larger doilies in half. Gather-stitch at folded edge to use as filler.

❖Using hat veiling, fold and stitch a 9"-wide bow near center of hat veiling. Hot-glue center of bow to back of porcelain shoulder plate. Drape and stitch remaining veiling around backside of wreath, allowing it to show a bit from wreath front.

❖Cut sheer mauve ribbon into a 36" length and a 45" length. Tie 36" length into a small 4"-wide bow with long tails. Stitch 45" length into a four-looped, 4"-wide bow. Drape and hot-glue single bow near top right side of wreath. Drape and hot-glue double bow near bottom left side of wreath. Randomly place and hot-glue old costume jewelry around wreath.

•Finishing

❖Trim stabilizer to fit around outside edges of porcelain doll head's shoulder plate. See (9). Hot-glue two ribbon loops to underside of stabilizer. Space ribbon loops 3" from center. Hot-glue stabilizer to wreath, small sections at a time.

Window Garland

Shown on page 80.
Materials

Thread: coordinating

Doilies: 1¾"-wide flower (4)

Wire: cloth-covered, 4 yds.

Flower spray stems: delicate, shell pink (6)

For Center Rose

Assorted ribbon: ¼"-wide satin, pale yellow, 3 yds.

Doily: 3"-diameter, crocheted; 4" all-over Battenburg (2); 4" Battenburg-edged; 6"-diameter crocheted heart

For Coral Spray

Assorted ribbon: 1½"-wide wired, apricot, ½ yd.

Doilies: 2" Battenburg square (2); 2" Battenburg heart (2)

For Wisteria Spray

Assorted ribbon: 1½"-wide grosgrain, ivory, 2½ yds.

For Gathered Rosebud

Assorted ribbons: 1½"-wide ombre, pale yellow/bright rose, 1 yd., for center of rosebuds; 1½"-wide wired, pale yellow, 1½ yds.

For Leaf Spray

Assorted ribbons: 1½"-wide wired sheer, lt. olive green, 2 yds.

Wire: cloth-covered, 6"

Florist tape: green or white

For Fuchsia

Silk ribbon: 4mm — lt. green, 1 yd.

Assorted ribbons: 1½"-wide peach, ¾ yd.; 1½"-wide coral, ⅜ yd.

Stamens: small gold-tipped (18)

For Bow/Greenery

Assorted ribbons: 1½"-wide sheer, lt. olive green, 4 yds.; 1"-wide sheer ombre, lt. olive green, 4 yds., (2 yds. to wrap entire garland and 2 yds. for stems)

Tools

Glue: hot glue gun and glue sticks

Needles: hand-sewing

Needlenose pliers

Pencil

Scissors: fabric

Ruler

Wire cutters

Directions

•Making Patterns and Cutting Fabrics

❖Using wire cutters, cut cloth-covered wire into thirteen 9" lengths and three 6" lengths. Save 6" lengths for leaf sprays. Using needlenose pliers, turn down one end of each 9" and 6" length of wire to form a loop. See (1).

❖Looped end of wire is top. Begin each flower by stitching looped end of wire to ribbon. See (2).

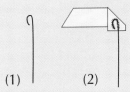

(1)   (2)

•Using Ribbons

❖Refer to General Instructions on pages 19-25.

❖Assemble all flower work following Flower Work and Embellishment Guide on page 87.

•Assembling

❖Refer to Placement Diagram on page 87. Assemble window garland following instructions below.

❖For center rose, knotted mum is attached to 9" wire. Slip wire through center of 3" crocheted doily. Place small amount of hot glue around wire onto doily. Slide knotted mum down to meet hot glue and squeeze doily up around knotted mum so doily ruffles slightly. Slip 4" all-over Battenburg doily onto wire, hot-glue, and ruffle. Add 4" Battenburg-edged doily in same manner. Gather-stitch around 6" crocheted heart doily so stitches are equally spaced from center with a 2"-diameter circle. Gather and secure thread. Wrap thread around gathered center several times. Trim excess doily to ¼" outside stitching. Slip wire through center of gathered heart doily and hot-glue to all in same manner. Finish with remaining 4" all-over Battenburg doily.

❖For first coral rose spray, one apricot gathered rosebud is attached to 9" wire. Fold 2" square Battenburg doily in half diagonally and slightly off center. Wrap around gathered rosebud. See (3). Fold second 6" length of ribbon in half, matching selvage edges. Gather-stitch along fold, tapering stitches at each end. Pull thread so gathered ribbon measures 1½". Wrap and stitch or glue ruffle around Battenburg doily. See (4). Slip wire through center of 2" Battenburg heart doily. Place small amount of hot glue around wire onto doily and squeeze doily up around ribbon ruffle so square doily ruffles slightly. See (5).

❖For second coral rose spray, one apricot gathered rosebud is attached to 9" wire. Fold 2" square Battenburg doily in half diagonally and slightly off center. Wrap around gathered rosebud. Slip wire through center of 2" Battenburg heart doily. Place small amount of hot glue around wire onto doily and squeeze doily up around gathered rosebud so heart doily ruffles slightly.

❖Twist the two coral rose sprays together. Twist these onto center rose wire so coral rose sprays are to right of center rose.

❖For wisteria sprays, twist one stem each onto center rose wire so one wisteria spray is to right and one is to left of center rose and coral rose spray cluster. Set remaining two wisteria sprays aside.

❖For rosebud center, attach 9" wire after first fold to each length for gathered rosebuds.

❖For rosebud outer, place gathered rosebud at center fold so top edge of rosebud is level with top edge of mountain folds. Wrap and stitch mountain folds around each rosebud. Secure thread. Repeat for each rosebud. Cover bottom edges of rosebud with 1"-wide sheer ombre lt. olive green ribbon to finish. Twist one gathered rosebud each onto garland to right and left of wisteria spray. Twist another wisteria spray and two more gathered rosebuds onto each side of garland.

❖For leaf sprays, glue three folded leaves each onto 6" of wire. Hide loop in-between layers of top leaf. Wrap with florist tape to hide raw edges. Make three leaf sprays and twist onto garland.

❖Wrap entire garland using 2 yds. 1"-wide sheer ombre lt. olive green ribbon for a more finished look. Arrange two sets of delicate flower spray stems together. Curl ends on pencil. Twist onto garland ends. Hot-glue four 1¾"-wide flower doilies to stems where needed for filler.

❖Cut four 12" lengths of 1½"-wide sheer lt. olive ribbon. Fold and stitch four two-looped bows. Cut one 12" length. Fold and stitch one four-looped bow. See (6).

❖Hot-glue center of one two-looped bow to stem between gathered rosebuds and wisteria at one end. Extend ribbon next to wisteria spray. Hot-glue second two-looped bow near wisteria spray. Extend ribbon to center rose. Repeat on opposite side.

❖Hot-glue four-looped bow behind center rose. Extend ribbon next to wisteria spray. Knot ribbon

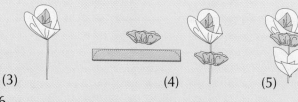

(3)   (4)   (5)

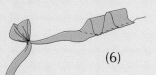

(6)

ends 10" from first and last bow. Cut ribbon just past knots.

❖Drape all fuchsias together. Stitch or hot-glue draped fuchsias to center of garland.

Window Garland • Flower Work and Embellishment Guide
Silk ribbons listed below are 4mm unless otherwise indicated.

Step		Ribbon Color	Flower Stitch
1	Center Rose	¼"-Wide Satin Pale Yellow	Knotted Mum
	❀Cut twenty 4" lengths. Make one knotted mum for center rose.		
2	Coral Spray	1½"-Wide Wired Apricot	Gathered Rosebud
	❀Cut three 6" lengths. Make two gathered rosebuds. The third 6" length is for ribbon ruffle.		
3	Flower	1½"-Wide Grosgrain Ivory	Wisteria Spray
	❀Cut twenty 5" lengths. Make four wisteria sprays with five petals on one wire, covering raw edges of previous petal with next petal.		
4	Rosebud, Center	1½"-Wide Ombre Pale Yellow/Bright Rose	Gathered Rosebud
	❀Cut six 6" lengths. Make six gathered rosebuds.		
5	Rosebud, Outer	1½"-Wide Wired Pale Yellow	Mountain Folds
	❀Fold ribbon into three mountain folds having each fold 2" deep on the double. Gather-stitch along bottom edge and pull thread to gather. Trim ribbon. Make a total of six.		
6	Leaf Spray	1½"-Wide Wired Sheer Lt. Olive Green	Folded Leaf
	❀Cut nine 4" lengths. Make nine folded leaves.		
7	Flower	1½"-Wide Peach, Lt. Green	Fuchsia
	❀Cut three 6" lengths peach ribbon. Make three fuchsias. Cut three 6" lengths lt. green ribbon for each fuchsia stem.		
8	Flower	1½"-Wide Coral, , Lt. Green	Fuchsia
	❀Cut three 6" lengths coral ribbon. Make three fuchsias. Cut three 6" lengths lt. green ribbon for fuchsia stem.		

❀*Additional Stitch Information*

Window Garland Placement Diagram

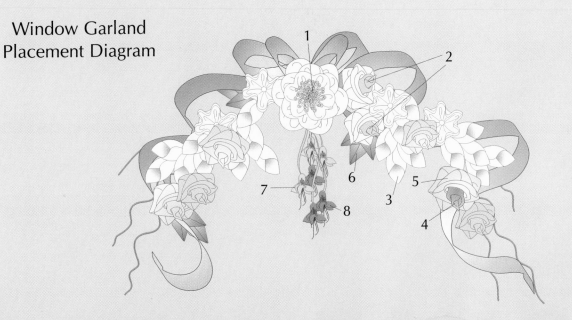

Cherub Pillow

Cherub Pillow

Materials

Fabric: moiré faille, ecru, ⅓ yd.

Thread: coordinating

Laces: small, assorted (5-10)

Silk ribbons: 4mm — pale green, 3 yds.;
ivory, taupe, off-white, 2 yds each;
7mm — ivory, taupe, 1½ yds each; off-
white, 1 yd.

Assorted ribbons: 9mm — pale green, ½
yd.; ivory, 1 yd.; 2mm — glitter-twill, pale
peach, 2 yds.

Embroidery floss: blush, ecru, pale gold,
ivory, lt. brown

Doily: 10"-diameter ecru, Battenburg

Charms: antique brass cupids (4)

Beads: small, pearl (18)

Pillow form: 10"

Tools

Glue: industrial-strength

Iron and ironing board

Needles: beading; chenille (size 20 and 22);
embroidery (size 7)

Marking tool

Scissors: fabric

Sewing machine

Directions

•Making Patterns and Cutting Fabrics

❖Using fabric scissors, cut a 12" square from ecru moiré faille for pillow front. Refer to Transfer Sheet on page 91. Center embroidery design on pillow front and mark location of heart shape.

•Assembling

❖Refer to General Instructions on pages 13-14.

❖Collage assorted laces onto pillow front up to outer edge of heart outline. Use a finished or turned under lace edge at heart outline. Overlap lace pieces ¼". Machine-stitch lace to pillow front using a narrow zigzag stitch, or hand-sew lace to pillow front with coordinating thread. Press.

•Embroidery

❖Refer to General Instructions on pages 14-25.

❖Refer to Transfer Sheet and Placement Diagram on page 91. Embroider design and assemble flower work following Ribbon Embroidery and Flower Work Color and Stitch Guide on page 90.

•Finishing

❖Trim pillow front to an 11" square. Cut an 11" square from ecru moiré faille for pillow back.

❖With right sides together, machine-stitch ½" seam leaving one side open. Trim bulk from corners. Turn right side out. Insert pillow form. Slip-stitch opening closed.

❖With right side up, center and pin 10" Battenburg doily underneath pillow. Slip-stitch doily to pillow back, up to pillow side seams.

(1)

❖Gather-stitch ½" to pillow corners. See (1). Gather each corner.

❖Cut 4mm ivory, off-white, taupe, and pale green silk ribbons into four 18" lengths each. Press if necessary. Layer a set of four shades together. Make a small bow at center of layered lengths. Repeat for remaining ribbon lengths for a total of four bows.

❖Stitch knot of bow to center of each puckered corner. Tie ribbon ends together, 4" from each bow. Trim ends to ½" below knot.

❖Using industrial-strength glue, attach antique brass cupids in each corner of pillow.

Cherub Pillow • Ribbon Embroidery and Flower Work Color and Stitch Guide

Silk ribbons listed below are 4mm unless otherwise indicated.
Embroidery floss listed below is three strands unless otherwise indicated.

Step		Ribbon and Floss Color	Stitch and Flower Stitch
1	Girl's Body	Blush Floss	Stem Stitch
2	Boy's Body	Ecru Floss	Stem Stitch
3	Wings	Ivory Floss	Stem Stitch
4	Girl's Hair	Ivory Floss	Couching Stitch
5	Boy's Hair	Pale Gold Floss	Couching Stitch
6	Facial Features	Lt. Brown Floss	Couching Stitch
7	Girl's Tiara	Lt. Brown Floss	Couching Stitch
8	Flower Stems	Lt. Brown Floss	Couching Stitch
9	Flower Stems	Pale Gold Floss	Couching Stitch
10	Rose Center	Ivory, 7mm	Ruffled Ribbon Stitch
	✿Stitch center ruffle of each rose that is deeper in shade.		
11	Rose Center	Off-White, 7mm	Ruffled Ribbon Stitch
	✿Stitch center ruffle of each rose that is palest in shade.		
12	Outer Ruffle	Taupe, 7mm	Ruffled Ribbon Stitch
	✿Stitch outer ruffle of each rose that is deeper in shade. Stitch outer ruffle layer of a pale rose.		
13	Textured Petals	Pale Peach Glitter-Twill	Zigzag Ruched Ribbon
	✿Fray end of ribbon. Pull a center fiber to ruche ribbon. Move gathers to meet fabric. Stitch into fabric at end of gathers to secure. Stitch small sprays, full circles and half circles. Tack with matching thread to shape stitches.		
14	Largest Leaves	Pale Green, 9mm	Loop Petal Stitch Variation
	✿Use larger chenille needle.		
15	Med. Leaves	Ivory, 9mm	Loop Petal Stitch Variation
	✿Use larger chenille needle.		
16	Smallest Leaves	Pale Green	Ribbon Stitch
	✿Tack center of ivory leaves with pale green leaves. Add additional pale green leaves around heart.		
17	Bouquet	Ivory, 7mm	French Knot
	✿Stitch very loose French Knots for flowers in bouquet.		
18	Bouquet	Off-White, 7mm	French Knot
	✿Stitch very loose French Knots.		
19	Bouquet	Taupe, 7mm	French Knot
20	Bouquet Leaves	Pale Green, 4mm	Ribbon Stitch
21	Beads	Pearls	Beading Stitch
	✿Stitch pearls where shown using beading needle. A variety of sizes can be used if desired.		
22	Bow	Pale Peach Glitter-Twill, 2mm	
	✿Cut 15" of ribbon. Tie bow near center. Stitch knot of bow to bouquet. Tack bow loops lightly. Tie knots in ribbon ends. Drape and tack knots.		

✿Additional Stitch Information

Cherub Pillow Transfer Sheet
Enlarge 200%

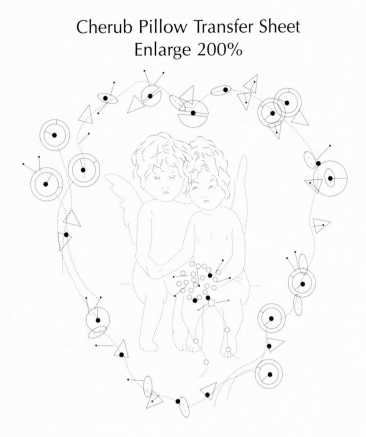

Cherub Pillow Placement Diagram

Rose Corsage

Hand Mirror

Crystal Jar Cover

Seashell Box

Rose Corsage

Materials

Doilies: 1½"-diameter, ecru, crocheted; 2½"-diameter, ecru, crocheted; 3"-diameter, ecru, crocheted; 4"-diameter, ecru, crocheted; 4"-diameter, ecru, Battenburg

Acrylic paint: pale lavender

Leaves: velvet, white/green, 2¼" (2)

Stamens: lavender and ivory, 6 each

Silk flower petals: to match stamens (4)

Pin back: 1½"

Tools

Cotton swabs

Paint dish: disposable

Glue: hot glue gun and glue sticks; industrial-strength

Scissors: craft

Textile medium

Directions

•Assembling

❖Refer to General Instructions on pages 11-14.

❖Paint all doilies, except 1½" doily, using pale lavender acrylic paint.

❖Using craft scissors, trim stamen ends so each is ¾" long. Hot-glue all stamens together at cut ends. Hot-glue stamen cluster to center of 2½" doily. Place thin bead of hot glue around cluster. Fold doily up around stamen cluster and squeeze around stamens so doily ruffles slightly.

❖At center of 3" doily, place thin bead of hot glue. Fold doily up around hot glue while gathering doily center so doily ruffles slightly. Hot-glue underside of 2½" doily to top center of 3" doily.

❖At center of 4" crocheted doily place thin bead of hot glue. Fold doily up around hot glue while gathering doily center so doily ruffles slightly. Hot-glue to underside of 3" doily.

❖At center of 4" Battenburg doily place thin bead of hot glue. Fold doily up around hot glue while gathering doily center so doily ruffles slightly. Hot-glue to left underside of 4" crocheted doily.

❖Hot-glue velvet leaves to left underside of corsage. Hot-glue silk flower petals to right underside of corsage.

•Finishing

❖Using industrial-strength glue, attach pin back slightly above center of corsage underside.

❖Open pin clasp. Hot-glue unpainted 1½" doily over pin back bar.

Hand Mirror

Materials

Fabric: back fabric, ivory, 6" square

Thread: coordinating

Silk ribbons: 7mm — pale peach, dusty purple, ½ yd. each

Assorted ribbons: 1"-wide ombre, lt. green/brown, ¼ yd.; 1"-wide ombre, lavender, ¾ yd.; ⅝"-wide satin, lt. olive green, ½ yd.; ⅜"-wide raspberry, 1¼ yds.; ⅞"-wide lavender, gold-edged ⅜ yd.; ¼"-wide velvet, mauve, 1¼ yds.

Lace: blush, 6" square

Trim: lettuce-edged, mauve, ¾ yd.; ⁵⁄₁₆"-wide ivory, ⅓ yd.; ½"-wide olive green, ½ yd.

Cording: ¼"-wide dk. olive green, ½ yd.; ½"-wide olive green, ½ yd.; ⁵⁄₁₆"-wide ivory, ⅓ yd.

Continued on page 94.

Continued from page 93.

Quilt batting: 5" x 5"

Cardboard: lightweight, 5" x 10"

Charm: antique brass cupid

Mirror: 4" x 4"

Tools

Glue: craft; hot glue gun and glue sticks; industrial-strength

Needles: hand-sewing

Marking tool

Ruler

Scissors: craft; fabric

Utility knife

Directions

•Making Patterns and Cutting Fabrics

❖Refer to General Instructions on pages 8-11.

❖See Hand Mirror Pattern on page 95. Using craft scissors, cut two hand mirror patterns from cardboard. Cut center from one cardboard piece to allow placement for mirror.

❖As alternative, trace outside shape of mirror onto cardboard, without handle. Add ⅟₁₆" around traced line. Cut out and label as top. Trace new shape onto cardboard. Measure inward ½" all around traced line. Cut opening with utility knife. Label as front.

❖Using fabric scissors, cut ivory fabric and blush lace ¾" larger than cardboard.

❖Place and label fabric cuts with corresponding cardboard pieces.

•Assembling

❖Refer to General Instructions on pages 11-12 and 15.

❖Using craft glue, glue ⁵⁄₁₆"-wide ivory cording to inside edge of mirror front to cover original mirror color. Glue ½"-wide olive green cording to mirror outer edge, continuing cording onto side edge of handle about ½".

❖Beginning at handle bottom end, diagonally wrap ⅝"-wide lt. olive green satin ribbon around handle, covering raw edges of cording at top of handle. Glue beginning and end of ribbon.

❖Pad mirror top with batting. Trim flush to edge and bevel inward slightly. Wrap with ivory fabric, clipping at curves. Trim bulk from points. Wrap lace over ivory fabric in the same manner.

❖Flute while hot-gluing ¼" mauve velvet ribbon to underside edge of mirror top. Hot-glue pad and wrapped cardboard top to mirror top.

❖Beginning at top point of mirror front cardboard, diagonally wrap ⅜"-wide raspberry ribbon around cardboard, beginning and ending on one side. This will be underside. It may be necessary to redirect diagonal angle to tightly wrap ribbon around cardboard. Continue until mirror front is completely covered.

❖Hot-glue edge of lettuce-edged trim to inside edge of mirror front. Hot-glue ribbon wrapped front to mirror front. Hot-glue ¼"-wide dk. olive green cording at mirror side edge between cardboard front and mirror front on outer edge.

•Using Ribbons

❖Refer to General Instructions on pages 19-25.

❖For mirror top, fold 1"-wide ombre lavender ribbon in half, matching cut ends. Stitch or hot-glue a narrow seam. Gather-stitch along darker ribbon edge. Pull gathers so inner circle measures 6" around. Gather-stitch along outer edge of ribbon. Pull gathers so outer circle measures 12" around. Hot-glue underside of inner circle edge to mirror top center.

❖Fold ⅞"-wide gold-edged ribbon in half, matching cut ends. Stitch or hot-glue narrow seam. Gather-stitch at one long edge. Tightly gather and secure thread. Gather-stitch ¼" inward from outer edge of ribbon. Pull gathers so outer circle measures 9" around. Hot-glue center underside of inner circle to center of outer ribbon layer.

❖Cut lt. green/brown ombre ribbon into two equal lengths. Make two Folded Leaves, having green edge at top. Hot-glue leaves together. Hot-glue to center left side of inner circle.

❖Gather-stitch remaining lettuce-edged trim along straight edge. Tightly gather and roll trim into a rose. Stitch on underside to hold rolls in place. Hot-glue to center ruffle.

❖Make a small bow using 7mm pale peach and dusty purple ribbons. Hot-glue knot of bow to top edge of handle.

❖Using industrial-strength glue, attach antique brass cupid over knot of bow.

Hand Mirror Pattern
Enlarge 200%

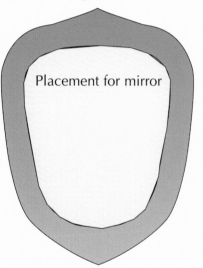

Placement for mirror

Hand Mirror Placement Diagram

Crystal Jar Cover

Shown on page 92.

Materials

Fabric: lid fabric, ivory, 5" piece

Thread: coordinating

Silk ribbon: 7mm — dusty purple, ⅜ yd.

Assorted ribbon: 1¼"-wide ombre, peach/mauve, ½ yd.

Trim: ½"-wide ivory, ⅓ yd.

Bugle beads: indigo (12)

Decorative beads: large, gold (5); large iridescent (4)

Seed beads: #10 — autumn, gold, metallic gold, mardi gras, mimosa, deep rose slate, sunset red, 1 package each

Quilt batting: 4" square

Doilies: 2"-diameter ecru, flower; 5" or 6" filet; 6" all-over Battenburg

Leaves: small velvet (3); small lt. olive green silk (2)

Wire: 22- and 26-gauge

Florist tape: green

Glass jar: small, with lid

Tools

Glue: craft; hot gun and glue sticks

Old paintbrush or 3" paint roller

Needles: hand sewing

Scissors: fabric

Wire cutters

Directions

•Assembling

❖Refer to General Instructions on pages 11-14.

❖Pad lid with quilt batting. Trim batting flush to jar lid and bevel inward slightly. Using craft glue and old paintbrush or 3" paint roller, tightly wrap ivory fabric around lid top and side. Trim excess fabric from bottom edge of lid side.

❖Using hot glue gun and glue stick, hot-glue trim over raw edge of ivory fabric, matching bottom edge of trim with bottom edge of lid side.

❖Center 6" all-over Battenburg doily on jar lid. Gather-stitch around doily at lid side. Tightly pull gathers and secure thread so doily fits tightly around lid. Place 5" or 6" filet doily over 6" all-over Battenburg doily. Hot-glue together at center top and around top edge of lid.

•Using Ribbons

❖Refer to General Instructions on pages 23-24.

❖Make a Pencil Violet using 7mm dusty purple ribbon.

❖Using wire cutters, cut required length of gauge wire. Assemble beaded flower and bead sprays following instructions below.

(1)   (2)   (3)

❖Make three petals using Rows 1-4 below. See (1).

❖Row 1: Use 4" length of 26-gauge wire. Place six mimosa, five gold metallic, and six mimosa. Twist ends of wire creating a loop.

❖Row 2: Use 4" length of 22-gauge wire. Place one large gold bead. Wire onto center of first loop.

❖Row 3: Use 4" length of 26-gauge wire. Place four mimosa, three gold metallic, three sunset red, five autumn, three sunset red, three gold metallic, and four mimosa. Twist ends of wire together creating a loop. Position around previous loop.

❖Row 4: Use 5" length of 26-gauge wire. Place one indigo bugle, three gold metallic, four sunset red, six autumn, eight mardi gras, seven slate, eight mardi gras, six autumn, four sunset red, three gold metallic, and one indigo bugle. Twist ends of wire together creating a loop. Position around previous loop. This completes the two smaller, middle petals. Continue with Row 5 for the third petal with an additional row.

❖Row 5: See (2). Use 5" length of 26-gauge wire. Place one indigo bugle, two gold metallic, three sunset red, five autumn, seven mardi gras, one deep rose, one mardi gras, one deep rose, one mardi gras, one deep rose, seven mardi gras, five autumn, three sunset red, two gold, and one indigo bugle. Twist ends of wire together creating loop. Position around previous loop. This completes third petal.

❖Make two petals using Rows 1-5 below. See (3).

❖Row 1: Use 4" length of 26-gauge wire. Place one indigo bugle, three deep rose, and one indigo bugle. Twist ends together creating loop.

❖Row 2: Use 4" length of 26-gauge wire. Place six sunset red, five autumn, and six sunset red. Twist ends together creating loop. Position around previous loop.

❖Row 3: Use 4" length of 26-gauge wire. Place one indigo bugle, three sunset red, four autumn, five mardi gras, four autumn, three sunset red, and one indigo bugle. Twist ends together creating loop. Position around previous loop.

❖Row 4: Use 4" length of 26-gauge wire. Place one indigo bugle, three sunset red, three autumn, five mardi gras, nine deep rose, five mardi gras, three autumn, three sunset red, and one indigo bugle. Twist ends together creating loop. Position around previous loop.

❖Row 5: Use 5" length of 26-gauge wire. Place one indigo bugle, two sunset red, three autumn, five mardi gras, seven deep rose, one slate, one deep rose, one slate, one deep rose, one slate, seven deep rose, five mardi gras, three autumn, two sunset red, and one indigo bugle. Twist ends together creating loop. Position around previous loop. This completes two petals. Twist these two petals onto three previous petals.

❖Make two bead sprays. For each, use 4" length of 22-gauge wire. Place two indigo bugle, one large iridescent, one indigo bugle, and one gold seed.

❖Make one bead spray. Use 4" length of 22-gauge wire. Place two indigo bugle, one large iridescent, one metallic gold, one indigo bugle, and one gold seed.

❖Make one bead spray. Use 4" length of 22-gauge wire. Place two gold bugle, one metallic gold, one gold bugle, and one gold seed.

❖Make one bead spray. Use 4" length of 22-gauge wire. Place two gold bugle, one large iridescent, one gold bugle, and one gold seed.

•Finishing

❖Attach assembled five beaded petals to 22-gauge wire. Twist five bead sprays onto beaded flower.

❖Wire leaves if necessary. Twist onto beaded flower.

❖Using 1¼"-wide peach/mauve ombre ribbon, fold and gather-stitch ribbon into a three-looped bow. Wire bow and twist onto beaded flower.

❖Wrap wired ends with florist tape. Fold wired ends under. Using craft glue, glue beaded flower to jar top center.

❖Hot-glue 2" doily to back side of beaded flower.

❖ Hot-glue pencil violet to middle of beaded flower.

Crystal Jar Cover Placement Diagram

Seashell Box

Shown on page 92.

Materials

Fabrics: outside fabric, off-white, ¼ yd.; inside fabric, off-white, 14" square

Silk ribbons: 4mm — three shades of off-white, ⅜ yd. each

Lace: ½"-wide French Valenciennes, 2"-wide off-white, crocheted, ¼ yd. each; ⅜"-wide off-white, crocheted, ⅝ yd.; 3½"-wide embroidered or eyelet, ¾ yd.

Trim: ½"-wide ecru, 1⅛ yd. or 1"-wide ecru, ⅝ yd.

Quilt batting: 7" square

Resin or porcelain ornament: 1½-2"-wide, off-white or any desired focal point item for center of box top

Seashells: small, off-white, pearl, or subtle color accent, six differently-shaped, depending on sizes, which range from ¼-¾", approximately 100 differently shaped shell are needed

Acrylic paint: off-white

Cardboard: lightweight, 7" x 14"

Papier mâché box: 6" emblem-shaped, with lid

Tools

Glue: craft, thin-bodied; hot glue gun and glue sticks; industrial-strength

Marking tool

Old paintbrush or 3" paint roller

Paintbrush

Ruler

Scissors: craft; fabric

Directions

•Making Patterns and Cutting Fabrics

❖Refer to General Instructions on pages 8-11.

❖Using papier mâché lid, trace lid onto cardboard. Using craft scissors, cut and label box lid.

❖Using papier mâché base, trace base onto cardboard adding ⅛". Cut and label one box base.

❖Using papier mâché box, measure diameter of inside. Cut and label a ⅜"-wide strip of cardboard ½" smaller than diameter of inside papier mâché box. Label as lining strip.

❖Using fabric scissors, cut outside fabric for lid and base, ¾" larger than cardboard box lid and cardboard box base.

❖Adding 1½" width and ½" length, measure and cut outside fabric for box sides.

❖Add ½" seam allowance. Cut inside fabric equal to inside bottom and side measurements for inside lining strip.

•Assembling

❖Refer to General Instructions on pages 11-12.

❖Using old paintbrush or 3" paint roller and thin-bodied craft glue, wrap and glue outside box fabric around cardboard base, cardboard lid, and box side.

❖Wrap 3½"-wide embroidered or eyelet lace around box side, placing lace ¾" above bottom edge of box. Using hot glue gun and glue stick, hot-glue ends of trim at center back of box side. Wrap unfinished edge of trim to inside of box. Hot-glue cardboard box base to box bottom.

❖Wrap and hot-glue embroidered or eyelet trim around top left side of cardboard lid. Wrap and hot-glue two rows of crocheted trim to top right side of cardboard lid.

❖Hot-glue ⅜"-wide lace to underside of cardboard lid, extending lace edge ⅛" past edge. Hot-glue cardboard lid to papier mâché box lid.

❖Cut quilt batting to fit inside box bottom and place inside on box bottom. Finger-gather fabric lining onto ⅜"-wide cardboard strip. Hot-glue lining to inside of box.

❖ Using paintbrush, paint inside of papier mâché box lid with off-white acrylic paint.

•Finishing

❖Refer to Placement Diagram below. Using thin-bodied craft glue, attach ¼"-sized pearl shells to bottom edge of papier mâché box, using cardboard base as a shelf for shells.

❖Cut a piece of cardboard smaller than focal point ornament. Hot-glue cardboard underneath ornament to raise ornament. Gather while hot-gluing ½"-wide lace trim to underside of focal point at top edge only. Using industrial-strength glue, attach ornament to center of box lid.

❖Arrange shells on box lid. Using craft glue, attach shells to box lid. Use pink-shaded shells minimally as filler.

❖Make a small bow using three shades of 4mm off-white ribbons. Hot-glue knot of bow to center top of focal point. Drape ribbon ends.

❖Hot-glue trim around edge of box lid.

Seashell Box Placement Diagram

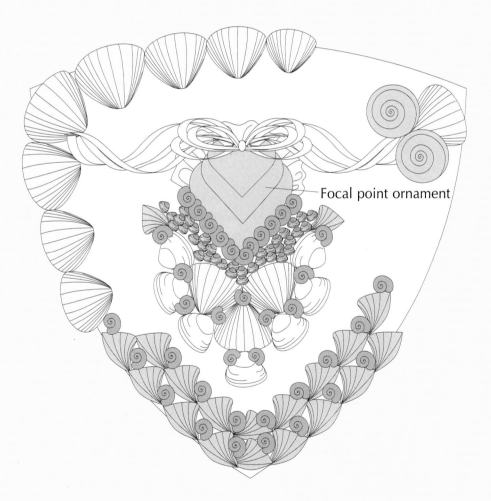

Focal point ornament

Victorian Purse

Antique Lace Pillow

Rose Garden Pillow

Nylon Bag

Victorian Purse

Materials

Fabric: of choice, ¼ yd., for lining

Thread: coordinating

Silk ribbons: 4mm — blush, pale pink, 1 yd. each; gray-green, dk. rose, 2 yds. each

Hand-dyed ribbons: darker rose, green, pale peach, lt. rose, 2 yds. each; mauve, 3 yds.

Lace: chantilly or lace of choice, large rose pattern, 9" x 22"

Trim: narrow, ½ yd., for inside

Seed beads: three shades of rose; olive-green, 1 small package each

Bugle beads: brown, 1 small package

Old pearls (25)

Purse frame: brass or vintage, 5"

Tools

Glue: craft

Iron and ironing board

Marking tool

Needles: beading; chenille (size 20)

Scissors: fabric

Sewing machine

Straight pins

Directions

•Making Patterns and Cutting Fabrics
❖Refer to General Instructions on pages 8-11.

❖Refer to Lace & Lining Pattern on page 102.

❖Add 1" seam allowance. Using fabric scissors, cut one front from chantilly lace, centering portion of lace design. Cut one inside front lining from fabric of choice.

❖Adding ¼" seam allowance cut one back from chantilly lace. Cut three linings from fabric of choice.

❖Layer and pin one purse lining under one chantilly lace front. Refer to Placement Diagram on page 102. Position diagram so rose is centered on layered lining and lace for purse front. Trace around pattern onto lace adding 1" seam allowance. Baste-stitch through lace and lining on seam allowance line. Cut lace and lining for front 1" larger than traced line.

•Embroidery
❖Refer to General Instructions on pages 14-19.

❖Embroider design following Ribbon Embroidery Color and Stitch Guide on page 102.

•Finishing
❖Trim purse front ¼" past baste stitching.

❖Layer and pin back lining under lace back.

❖With right sides together, machine-stitch embroidered front lace and lining to outside back lace and lining with ¼" seam allowance. Stitch to side marks shown on Lace and Lining Pattern on page 102. Turn right side out. Press, avoiding embroidery.

❖With right sides together, machine-stitch purse front lining to purse back lining with ¼" seam allowance. Stitch to side marks shown on Lace and Lining Pattern on page 102.

❖With right sides together, slip purse outside over lining, aligning top raw edges. Stitch ¼" seam, leaving an opening for turning at purse back top edge as shown on Lace and Lining Pattern on page 102.

❖Turn purse right side out through opening. Press top seam flat. Hand-stitch opening closed.

❖Gather-stitch along top edges of purse front and back as shown on Lace and Lining Pattern on page 102 so purse fabric fits brass frame. Secure gather stitches when properly sized.

❖Hand-stitch purse to frame through frame stitch holes. Stitch beads over hand stitching to cover stitching threads. Use frame holes to anchor beads to frame.

❖Using craft glue on inside of purse, glue narrow trim to inside top edge to cover hand stitching.

Victorian Purse • Ribbon Embroidery Color and Stitch Guide
Silk ribbons listed below are 4mm unless otherwise indicated.

Step		Ribbon Color	Stitch
1	Large Rose	Pale Peach (hand-dyed)	Ribbon Stitch
2	Large Rose	Lt. Rose (hand-dyed)	Ribbon Stitch
3	Large Rose	Darker Rose (hand-dyed)	Ribbon Stitch
4	Large Rose	Pale Pink	Ribbon Stitch
5	Large Rose	Blush	Ribbon Stitch
6	Large Rose	Dk. Rose	French Knot, Ribbon Stitch
7	Large Rose	Pale Peach (hand-dyed)	French Knot
8	Small Flowers	Mauve (hand-dyed)	Ribbon Stitch
9	Leaves	Green (hand-dyed)	Ribbon Stitch
10	Leaves	Gray-Green	Ribbon Stitch
11	Stems	Alternate Brown Bugle Beads and Olive Green Seed Beads	Beading Stitch
12	Flower Centers	Old Pearls	Beading Stitch
13	Rose Highlights	Rose Seed Beads	Beading Stitch

Victorian Purse Placement Diagram

Victorian Purse Lace & Lining Pattern
Enlarge 275%

Gather-stitch between these marks

Leave open for turning

Stitch to here   Stitch to here

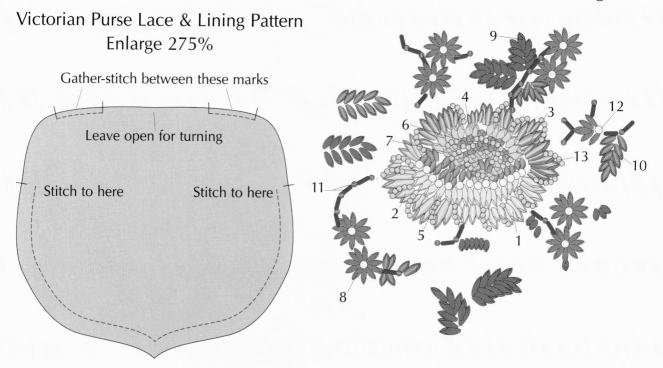

Antique Lace Pillow

Shown on page 100.

Materials

Fabrics: pillow front fabric, 11" x 22"; pillow back fabric, ⅓ yd.; voile or organdy, ecru, ½ yd.; muslin, ⅓ yd.

Thread: coordinating

Silk ribbons: 4mm — blush, 3 yds.; cafe, ivory, 2½ yds. each; lavender/violet, pale green, taupe, 2 yds. each; pale peach, 3½ yds.; 7mm — ecru, ⅜ yd.; ivory, ¾ yd.; pale peach, 2 yds.

Hand-dyed ribbon: green, 2½ yds.

Assorted ribbon: ½"-wide grosgrain, pale peach, ½ yd.

Embroidery floss: lt. green

Lace: piece of treasure lace, or any desired lace piece

Stuffing: polyester

Tools

Iron and ironing board

Marking tool

Needles: chenille (size 20); hand-sewing

Scissors: fabric

Sewing machine

Directions

•Making Patterns and Cutting Fabrics

❖Refer to General Instructions on pages 8-11.

❖Refer to Transfer Sheet and Placement Diagram on page 104. Transfer design to pillow front fabric.

❖Place lace piece on pillow front below embroidery location. Mark lace placement and baste-stitch on placement lines.

•Embroidery and Using Ribbons

❖Refer to General Instructions on pages 14-25.

❖Embroider design onto pillow front fabric following Ribbon Embroidery Color and Stitch Guide on page 104.

•Finishing

❖Hand-stitch lace to pillow front. Remove baste stitch.

❖Using fabric scissors, cut two 11" x 15" pieces of fabric for pillow back. Fold and press one short edge of pillow back fabric over 1". Fold over again on itself and press. Machine-stitch fold in place. Repeat for second pillow back piece.

❖Taper pillow corners to eliminate bulk in corners.

❖For pillow ruffle, cut 4"-wide bias strips from voile or organdy fabric for a total of 150". Stitch ends together, then join ends to form a circle. Press seams open. Fold bias strip in half, matching long edges. Do not press fold. Machine-gather-stitch ½" from raw edges. Machine-gather-stitch again ⅛" away from first row. Pull gathers to fit pillow front outer edge. Pin in place onto right side of pillow front. Machine-stitch ruffle to pillow front.

❖With right sides together, overlap and pin pillow backs onto pillow front. Machine-stitch together, taking ½" seam. Do not catch edges of ruffle in seam. Trim bulk from corners and trim seam to ¼". Zigzag-stitch raw edges. Turn right side out.

❖Cut muslin 11" x 44" for pillow form. Fold in half, matching 11" sides. Stitch along two long edges, taking ¼" seam. Turn right side out. Using polyester stuffing, stuff form. Machine-stitch opening closed.

❖Insert into lace pillowcase.

Antique Lace Pillow • Ribbon Embroidery Color and Stitch Guide

Silk ribbons listed below are 4mm unless otherwise indicated.
Embroidery floss listed below is three strands unless otherwise indicated.

Step		Ribbon and Floss Color	Stitch and Flower Stitch
1	Flower	Pale Peach Grosgrain	Pansy
	✿Cut three 5" lengths. Make three pansies.		
2	Stems	Lt. Green Floss	Couching Stitch
3	Large Buds	Ecru, 7mm	Cross-over Lazy Daisy
4	Ruffles	Taupe	Ruffled Ribbon Stitch
	✿Stitch Ruffled Ribbon Stitches at base of three of large buds and each pansy center.		
5	Petals	Pale Peach	1-Twist Ribbon Stitch
	✿Stitch petals at sides of large buds.		
6	Leaves	Cafe	Bullion Lazy Daisy (2 wraps)
7	Sprays	Blush	Loop Petal Stitch
8	Sprays	Pale Peach	Loop Petal Stitch
9	Sprays	Ivory	Ribbon Stitch
10	Leaves	Pale Green	Lazy Daisy
11	Leaves	Green (hand-dyed)	Ribbon Stitch, 1-Twist Ribbon Stitch
12	Color Splash	Lavender/Violet	Ribbon Stitch
13	Twigs	Cafe	Cascade Stitch
14	Bow	Ecru, Ivory, 7mm	Pencil Violet
	✿Cut two 24" lengths from ivory and one 24" length from ecru. Make two pencil violets from ivory ribbon and one from ecru ribbon. Stitch center of each pencil violet to outer corners of embroidery. Knot ribbon ends.		

✿Additional Stitch Information

Antique Lace Pillow Transfer Sheet
Enlarge 240%

Antique Lace Pillow Placement Diagram

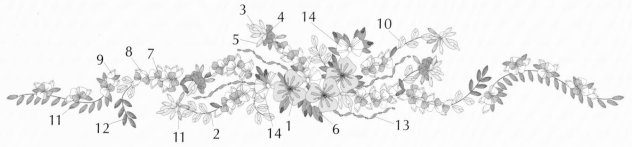

Rose Garden Pillow

Shown on page 100.

Materials

Fabrics: brocade, ½ yd.; decorator stripe, coordinating color, ½ yd.; muslin, ⅜ yd., for pillow form, or purchase 11" x 17" pillow form

Thread: coordinating

For Garden Rose

Assorted ribbon: 1½"-wide wired, pale pink, 2¾ yds.

Stamens: gold-tipped, small bunch

Wire: cotton-covered, 6"

For Single Petal Rose

Assorted ribbons: ⅞"-wide sheer ombre, peach/lt. green/ivory, 2¾ yds.

For Double-edge Gathered Rose

Assorted ribbons: 1½"-wide wired, peach, 1 yd.; ⅞"-wide wired cross-dyed, orange/green, ⅔ yd.

For Rosette

Assorted ribbon: ⅝"-wide, pale mauve, ½ yd.

For Leaves

Assorted ribbons: 1½"-wide wired, lt green, ⅝ yd., for gathered leaves; ⅞"-wide ombre, lt. green/brown, ¾ yd., for gathered leaves; ⅞"-wide satin-edged, dk. green, 1 yd., for folded leaves

For Pillow

Silk ribbons: 7mm — ecru, 2 yds.; gold, 3 yds.; gray-green, 1½ yds.; pale peach, 2½ yds.

Hand-dyed ribbons: 4mm — green, 1½ yds.; 7mm — yellow/gold, 2 yds.

Assorted ribbon: textured, lavender, ¾ yd.; 1.5 textured ribbon, pale peach, 2 yds.

Embroidery floss: gray-green, pine green

Lace: scalloped edge, ⅝ yd.

Doily: 6"-diameter

Cording: ¼"-wide ivory, 1¾ yds.

Stuffing: polyester

Tools

Glue: hot glue gun and glue sticks

Iron and ironing board

Marking tool

Needles: hand-sewing

Needlenose pliers

Ruler

Scissors: fabric

Sewing machine

Straight pins

Wire cutters

Directions

•Making Patterns and Cutting Fabrics

❖Using fabric scissors, cut brocade fabric 13" x 19" for pillow front.

•Assembling

❖Overlay and hand-stitch scalloped lace over fabric so scalloped edge is 1¼" away from one long edge. This is pillow's bottom edge. Machine- or hand-stitch 6" doily onto pillow front.

•Embroidery and Using Ribbons

❖Refer to General Instructions on pages 14-25.

❖Refer to Transfer Sheet on page 106. Transfer design to pillow front fabric.

❖Embroider design following steps 1-10 on Embroidery and Flower Work Color and Stitch Guide on page 107.

❖Assemble all flower work following steps 11-19 on Embroidery and Flower Work Color and Stitch Guide on page 107.

•Finishing

❖Refer to Placement Diagram below. Using hot glue gun and glue stick, hot-glue or stitch flower work to pillow front.

❖Cut two 12" x 13" pieces from stripe fabric, for pillow back. Fold and press one short edge of pillow back fabric over 1". Fold over again on itself and press. Machine-stitch fold in place. Repeat for second pillow back piece. Taper pillow corners to eliminate bulk. With right sides together, overlap and pin pillow backs onto pillow front. Machine-stitch together, taking ½" seam. Turn right side out.

❖Hand-stitch cording at outer edge of pillow side seams.

❖Cut muslin fabric 11" x 17" for pillow form. With right sides together, machine-stitch, leaving an opening. Turn and stuff with polyester stuffing. Stitch opening closed.

❖Insert into pillowcase.

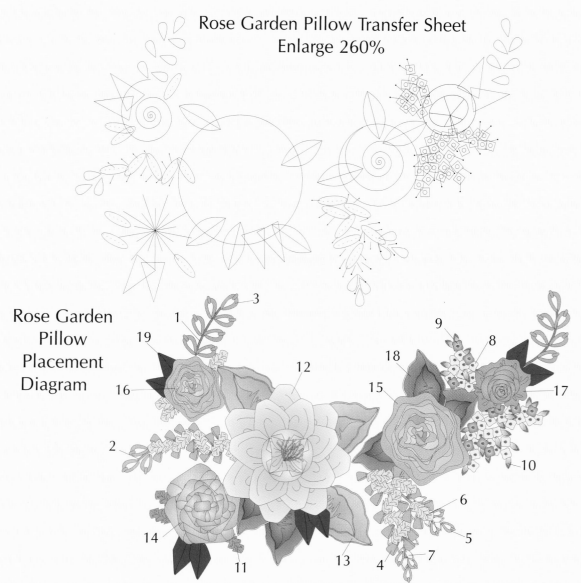

Rose Garden Pillow Transfer Sheet
Enlarge 260%

Rose Garden Pillow Placement Diagram

Rose Garden Pillow • Embroidery and Flower Work Color and Stitch Guide

Silk ribbons listed below are 4mm unless otherwise indicated.
Embroidery floss listed below is three strands unless otherwise indicated.

Step		Ribbon and Floss Color	Stitch and Flower Stitch
1	Stems	Pine Green Floss	Stem Stitch
2	Stems	Gray-Green Floss	Stem Stitch
3	Leaf Sprays	Gray-Green, 7mm	Lazy Daisy
4	Snapdragons, Blooming	Gold (hand-dyed), 7mm	Loop Petal Stitch
5	Snapdragons, Buds	Gold (hand-dyed), 7mm	Lazy Daisy
6	Snapdragons	Pale Peach, 7mm	Zigzag Ruched Ribbon

❀Fray end of ribbon. Pull a center fiber to ruche ribbon. Move gathers to meet fabric. Stitch into fabric at end of gathers to secure. Stitch in-between Loop Petal Stitches for blooming snapdragons.

7	Snapdragons	Ivory	Ribbon Stitch, 1-Twist

❀Stitch in-between buds on two stems.   Ribbon Stitch

8	Baby's Breath	Ecru, 7mm	Tacked Loop Stitch

❀Tack each bloom with French Knot, using either gray-green or pine green floss.

9	Baby's Breath	Gold, 7mm	Tacked Loop Stitch

❀Tack each bloom with French Knot, using either gray-green or pine green floss.

10	Baby's Breath	Green (hand-dyed)	Ribbon Stitch
11	Heather Texture	Dusty Purple Textured	Zigzag Ruched Ribbon

❀Fray end of ribbon. Pull a center fiber to ruche ribbon. Move gathers to meet fabric. Stitch into fabric at end of gathers to secure.

12	Flower	1½"-Wide Wired Pale Pink	Garden Rose

❀Cut eight 4" lengths, eight 4½" lengths, and five 5" lengths. Make one garden rose. Do not wire. Stitch garden rose over largest leaves. Push fingers down, in, and around petals to cup them properly. Stitch some petals to fabric near base of petals.

13	Leaves	1½"-Wide Lt. Green Wired	Gathered Leaf

❀Cut three 7" lengths. Make three gathered leaves. Stitch in place under garden rose, stitching leaf edges down for texture.

14	Flower	⅞"-Wide Sheer Ombre Ivory/Lt. Green/Peach	Single Petal Rose

❀Make one single petal rose. Stitch in place.

15	Flower	1½"-Wide Peach Wired	Double-edge Gathered Rose

❀Make one double-edge gathered rose. Stitch in place.

16	Flower	⅞"-Wide Cross-dyed Wired Orange/Green	Double-edge Gathered Rose

❀Make one double-edge gathered rose. Stitch in place.

17	Flower	Pale Mauve, 15mm	Rosette

❀Make one rosette. Stitch in place.

18	Leaves	⅞"-Wide Lt. Green/Brown Ombre	Gathered Leaf

❀Cut five 5" lengths. Make five gathered leaves. Stitch in place under each double-edge gathered rose and garden rose.

19	Leaves	⅞"-Wide Dk. Green Satin-edged	Folded Leaf

❀Cut eight 4½" lengths. Make eight folded leaves. Stitch in place scattered among flower work. Stitch tips of leaves to fabric.

❀*Additional Stitch Information*

Nylon Bag

Shown on page 100.
Materials

Fabric: satin, pale blue, 9" x 15"

Assorted ribbons: ⅝"-wide ombre, lavender/blue, 1⅜ yds.; ⅝"-wide ombre, lavender/green, 1¼ yds.; ⅞"-wide satin, pale blue, 1½ yds.; 1½"-wide ombre, pale rose/green, 1⅜ yds.

Thread: coordinating

Cording: narrow, blue, 1⅛ yds.

Garland: lt. green/blue buds and bow, 2¼ yds.; lt. blue/white buds and bow, 1¼ yds.

Lace: 1½"-wide French Valenciennes, ½ yd.

Netting: 6" x 24"

Tools

Needles: hand-sewing

Scissors: fabric

Sewing machine

Directions

•Making Patterns and Cutting Fabrics
❖Refer to General Instructions on pages 8-11.

❖Using fabric scissors, cut two 12" lengths from satin pale blue ribbon. Cut ombre pale rose/green ribbon into two 24" lengths. Cut netting into two 3" x 24" lengths. Cut ombre lavender/blue ribbon into two 24" lengths.

•Assembling
❖Machine-gather-stitch one 24" length pale rose/green ombre ribbon at pale rose edge. Adjust gathers to fit one long edge of 12" satin pale blue ribbon. With right sides together, place satin pale blue ribbon on top of gathered edge of ombre pale

rose/green ribbon. Machine-stitch ribbons together with a narrow zigzag, creating a ¹⁄₁₆"-wide seam. See (1).

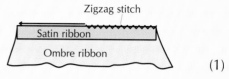

(1)

❖Repeat this process for remaining pale rose/green ombre ribbon and satin pale blue ribbon.

❖Machine-stitch lt. green/blue buds and bow garland over seamed edges.

❖Overlap selvage edge of ombre pale rose/green ribbon ¼" onto one long edge of netting. Machine-stitch together with a narrow zigzag. Repeat for opposite side of ombre ribbon with remaining netting strip. Machine-stitch lt. green/blue buds and bow garland over seamed edges. See (2).

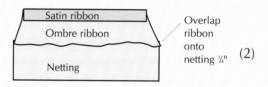

(2)

❖Overlap selvage edge of ombre lavender/ blue ribbon ¼" onto long edge of netting. Machine-stitch together with a narrow zigzag. Repeat for opposite side of ombre ribbon with remaining long edge of netting. See (3).

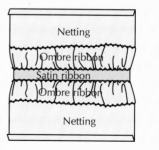

(3)

❖With wrong sides together, fold entire piece of ombre ribbon and netting in half, matching raw edges at top and ombre ribbon selvage edges at sides. Using a narrow zigzag, machine-stitch selvage edges of ombre ribbon together. See (4). Machine-stitch lt. blue/white buds and bow garland over outer selvage edge of ombre ribbon.

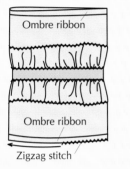

(4)

❖With right sides together, fold 9" x 15" piece of satin fabric in half, matching 9" lengths at top. Trim bottom to curve slightly. See (5). With a ¼" seam allowance, machine-stitch, leaving top straight edge open. This is bag lining.

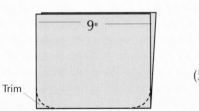

(5)

❖With right sides together, slip lining over ribbon bag. With ¼" seam allowance, machine-stitch top edges of stripped ribbon piece to top edges of lining, leaving an opening. See (6). Turn bag right side out through opening. Press top seam. Hand-stitch opening closed.

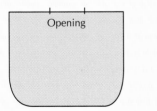

(6)

❖Fold 1½"-wide lace in half lengthwise, matching cut ends. Stitch ¼" seam. Press seam open.

❖Using a narrow zigzag, machine-stitch edge of lace to top finished edge of bag, matching edges.

❖Cut ombre lavender/green ribbon into two 9" lengths. Fold each cut end under ¼". Place one length of ribbon at top, finished edge of bag, aligning folded ribbon ends at side seams. Machine-stitch in place with narrow zigzag. Repeat for remaining length of ribbon, on opposite side of bag. Machine-stitch bottom edges of ombre lavender/green ribbon onto bag, creating casing. See (7).

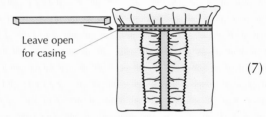

(7)

•**Using Ribbons**

❖Refer to General Instructions on pages 19-25.

❖Make four Rosettes by cutting remaining pale blue satin ribbon into four equal lengths. Stitch each length into a rosette, eliminating the ruffle.

•**Finishing**

❖Cut cording in half. Insert one piece of cording through left side of casing opening, going around bag. Tie cording ends together, then move cording so knot is hidden within casing. Repeat for right side casing.

❖Gather-stitch bottom folded edge of bag into center. Tightly gather and secure thread. Tack bottom center of lining to center of ribbon bag.

❖Tack a rosette to each top side edge, center, and at bottom center of bag.

Wall Pocket

Materials

Fabric: tan, ½ yd.

Thread: coordinating

Cording: narrow, ivory, 2 yds.

Silk ribbons: 4mm — blush, mauve, 1 yd. each; 7mm — mauve, ½ yd.; 32mm — tan, ¾ yd.

Assorted ribbons: ⅛"-wide grosgrain dk. tan, 1 yd.; ½"-wide grosgrain, ivory, 1"-wide metallic, antique gold, ½ yd. each; 1½"-wide ivory, ⅔ yd.

Hand-dyed ribbon: ⅜"-wide velvet, mauve, ¾ yd.

Embroidery floss: ivory

Lace: lace or netting: small pieces, (8-10)

Trim: braided, ecru, ¾ yd.

Stuffing: polyester, (small amount)

Quilt batting: 9" square

Seed beads: bronze, lt. coral, iridescent gold, metallic gold

Bronze beads: large (8)

Stamens: small (12)

Leaves: velvet or satin, small (32)

Double-sided fusible web: 2" x 14"

Acrylic paint: flesh; sage green, for eyes; ivory and lt. rose, for dress; metallic gold and brown, for hair; bright rose, for lips and cheeks; iridescent pearl

Cardboard: heavy, ½ sheet

Tools

Glue: hot glue gun and glue sticks

Fabric pen: fine-point, brown

Iron and ironing board

Marking tool

Needles: embroidery (size 7); hand-sewing

Paintbrush: fine-point

Textile medium

Paint pallet

Ruler

Scissors: fabric; craft

Tape measure

Water

Directions

•Making Patterns and Cutting Fabrics

❖Refer to General Instructions on pages 8-11.

❖Refer to Wall Pocket Patterns on page 114. Using craft scissors, cut one front, one inside front, one back, and one inside back from cardboard.

❖Add ¾" seam allowance. Using fabric scissors cut inside front, one back, and one inside back from tan fabric. Cut one 9" x 9" square from tan fabric for front. Cut one 2" x 28" from tan fabric. Cut one 2" x 14" strip from double-sided fusible web for side strip. See (1).

❖Place and label fabric cuts with corresponding cardboard pieces.

•Assembling

❖Refer to General Instructions on pages 11-14.

❖Using hot glue gun and glue stick, snugly wrap and hot-glue tan fabric for back around one cardboard back piece. Clip curves as necessary. Trim bulk at bottom point. Repeat for inside back piece.

❖Wrap and hot-glue tan fabric for inside front around one cardboard piece. Clip curves as necessary. Trim bulk at bottom point.

❖Press under short ends of 2" x 28" tan strip. Apply double-sided fusible web to middle of strip, following manufacturer's instructions. See (1). Peel off fusible web backing. Fold ends of strip over to meet at center. Fuse in place. Trim fabric to measure 1" wide at center. Mark center of strip. See (2).

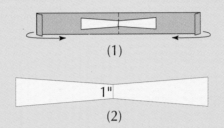

(1)

(2)

❖Using tape measure, beginning at center bottom of inside back, measure around curve 7" up side of back piece. Repeat for other side. Marks should be directly across from each other. Hot-glue ¼" of side strip to underside edge of inside back wall pocket, beginning at center bottom. End side strip at marks. Measure 7" up from side of inside front. Hot-glue ¼" of remaining raw edge of side strip to underside edge of inside front, in same manner as inside back, creating the "pocket".

❖Cut a 4" piece of narrow ivory cording. Loop cording and hot-glue to center top of wall pocket back on underside. This will be hanger for wall pocket. With wrong sides together, hot-glue back to inside back. Hot-glue braided ecru trim to top of back wall pocket.

❖Refer to Transfer Sheet and Angel Diagram on page 114. Trace heart front onto wrong side of 9" x 9" square tan fabric. Baste-stitch on traced line.

❖With right side up, transfer angel design on front of 9" x 9" square tan fabric.

❖Using fine-point paintbrush and each shade of acrylic paint, place a dab of each shade of acrylic paint into a paint pallet. Thin each shade of paint with an equal amount of textile medium. Add drops of water to thin more, if needed. Mix paints as needed to create more colors.

❖Paint angel, working up to transfer marks. Let paint dry thoroughly. Add detail to angel with brown fine-point fabric pen.

❖Hand-stitch a flat layer of lace or netting directly over angel for softening effect.

❖Collage and stitch remaining lace or netting onto front fabric. Pleat lace or netting pieces to create textured appearance. Place and stitch lace or netting pieces directly up to angel.

•**Embroidery**

❖Refer to General Instructions on pages 14-25.

❖Refer to Transfer Sheet and Placement Diagram on page 114. Embroider and bead angel following steps 1-6 on Ribbon Embroidery and Flower Work Color and Stitch Guide on page 113.

•**Finishing**

❖Make bow using ⅜"-wide mauve velvet ribbon. Drape bow on front of wall pocket. Hand-stitch in place.

❖Pad remaining cardboard front with quilt batting. Trim flush to edge beveling inward slightly. Trim angel and lace piece to ¾" outside basting line. Center and wrap angel piece around padded cardboard.

❖With wrong sides together, hot-glue front to inside front. Hot-glue velvet leaves around outer edge of embellished front.

❖Assemble all flower work following steps 7-13 on Ribbon Embroidery and Flower Work Color and Stitch Guide on page 113.

❖Stitch a multi-looped bow with 18" tails from narrow ivory cording. Hot-glue knot of bow under 7mm mauve rosette at top left edge of wall pocket. Drape and swirl cording ends. Tack in place using four large bronze beads.

❖Hot-glue two velvet leaves to back piece behind knotted half-mum.

❖Make one Circular Ruffle using remaining 1"-wide antique gold metallic ribbon. Ruffle will be used to cover hanger for wall pocket.

❖Fold remaining ⅜"-wide velvet ribbon in half. Tie knot 1" down from fold, forming a loop. Hot-glue over center back of 1"-wide antique gold metallic circular ruffle. Hot-glue two velvet leaves to side of circular ruffle. Hot-glue to center top of wall pocket back to hide 4" piece of narrow ivory cording hanger.

Wall Pocket • Ribbon Embroidery and Flower Work Color and Stitch Guide

Silk ribbons listed below are 4mm unless otherwise indicated.
Embroidery floss listed below is three strands unless otherwise indicated.

Step		Ribbon and Floss Color	Stitch and Flower Stitch
1	Flower	Blush	French Knot
2	Flower	Blush	Ribbon Stitch
3	Flower	Mauve	Bullion Lazy Daisy
4	Flower	Mauve, 7mm	Ribbon Stitch
5	Beads		Beading Stitch
6	Outline	Ivory Floss	Stem Stitch
7	Pointed Petal Flower	Tan, 32mm	Dahlia, Double Fold
	❁Cut seven 3¼" lengths. Do not join first petal to last petal. Make one half dahlia. Hot-glue pointed petal flower to top left edge of heart above angel.		
8	Flower	⅛"-Wide Grosgrain Dk. Tan	Knotted Half-Mum
	❁Cut twelve 2½" lengths. Make one knotted half-mum. Hot-glue knotted half-mum over center of pointed petal flower.		
9	Berries	1½"-Wide Ivory	Berry
	❁Cut nine 1½" lengths. Make nine berries. Use a beading needle, stitch bronze seed bead to center top of each berry. Hot-glue berries to left side of heart under pointed petal flower.		
10	Flower, Outer	½"-Wide Grosgrain Ivory	Folded Petal
	❁Cut seven 2" lengths. Make seven folded petals. Overlap, while hot-gluing on lower right of pocket, folded petals in a semi-circle.		
11	Flower	1½"-Wide Ivory	Turban
	❁Using remaining ivory ribbon, make one turban. Stitch one large bronze bead to center of turban. Hot-glue turban over center of folded petals.		
12	Flower	1"-Wide Metallic Antique Gold, Mauve	Fuchsia
	❁Cut three 4" lengths metallic antique gold ribbon. Make three fuchsias. Cut 6" length mauve ribbon for fuchsia stems. Hot-glue four stamens to inside center of each fuchsia. Drape and hot-glue fuchsias in place at top right edge of wall pocket. Tack stems in place using three large bronze beads.		
13	Rose	Mauve, 7mm	Rosette
	❁Cut two 9" lengths. Make two rosettes. Cut two 4½" lengths. Hot-glue one rosette over center of knotted half-mum. Hot-glue second rosette to top right edge of turban.		

❁*Additional Stitch Information*

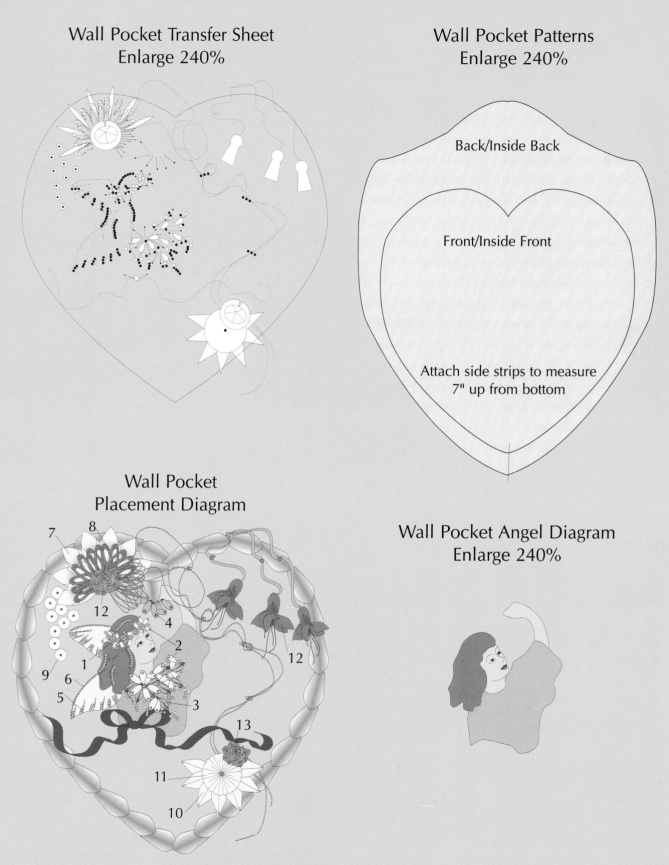

Wall Pocket Transfer Sheet
Enlarge 240%

Wall Pocket Patterns
Enlarge 240%

Back/Inside Back

Front/Inside Front

Attach side strips to measure
7" up from bottom

Wall Pocket
Placement Diagram

7

8

12

4

2

1

9

6

5

3

13

11

10

12

Wall Pocket Angel Diagram
Enlarge 240%

Pincushion Box

Wool Pillow

Powder Puff

Oval Box

Pincushion Box

Shown on page 115.

Materials

Fabrics: inside fabric, wine, 9" x 13"; outside fabric, velvet, olive green, 9" x 8"

Thread: coordinating

Silk ribbons: 4mm — olive green, ¾ yd.; wine, dk. wine, ½ yd. each

Assorted ribbons: ⅝"-wide satin, olive green, ⅛ yd.; ¼"-wide velvet, wine, ½ yd.; 1"-wide sheer, hunter green, ¼ yd.

Lace: ½"-wide, dk. ecru, ¼ yd.

Stuffing: polyester (handful)

Quilt batting: 2" x 5"

Beads: variety of medium-sized (4)

Charms: antique brass hand mirrors, small (2)

Corsage pins: (2)

Cabbage: velvet, small (or any other 9-petal velvet item)

Cardboard: heavy, 12" x 3"; lightweight, 8" x 4"

Dowel: wooden 1"-diameter

Tools

Glue: hot glue gun and glue sticks; industrial-strength

Marking tool

Needles: hand-sewing; heavyweight

Ruler

Scissors: craft; fabric

Sewing machine

Toothpicks

Directions

•Making Patterns and Cutting Fabrics

❖Refer to General Instructions on pages 8-11.

❖Refer to Pincushion Box Patterns on page 118.

❖Using craft scissors, cut one box side and one lining strip from lightweight cardboard. Cut one lid and base, one middle lid, one inside lid, and one inside bottom from heavy cardboard.

❖Using fabric scissors, cut one inside box bottom lining from inside fabric. Cut one top fabric 2" x 7" from inside fabric.

❖Cut one box side 3½" x 8" from outside fabric. Cut one lid and base (3" circle) and one middle lid (3¼" circle) from outside fabric. Cut one inside lid (2½" circle) from inside fabric.

❖Place and label fabric cuts with corresponding cardboard pieces.

•Assembling

❖Refer to General Instructions on pages 11-13.

❖Laminate box side cardboard with outside velvet fabric. Laminate outside fabric around cardboard base and middle lid.

❖Trim excess fabric from corners of box side.

❖With wrong side down, place box side cardboard on work surface. Using a round hot glue stick, or anything similar in diameter, roll box side covered cardboard into circular shape.

❖Lightly hot-glue quilt batting to inside lid. Trim batting flush to cardboard's edge and bevel inward slightly. Wrap inside lid fabric around inside lid.

❖Fold top fabric in half, matching short edges. Machine- or hand-sew ¼" seam at short edges. Finger press seam open. Turn right side out. Hot-glue ¼" fabric edge to underside edge of cardboard lid, beginning at seam. At opposite edge of cardboard lid, hot-glue fabric edge to underside edge of cardboard lid. Continue to hot-glue fabric edge to remaining edges of cardboard lid, creating a cup of fabric with a cardboard base. Turn fabric cup side up.

❖Using polyester stuffing, stuff fabric cup firmly. Turn under remaining long edge of fabric cup while gather-stitching along folded edge. Tightly gather to close cup and secure thread.

❖Inside bottom is not wrapped with fabric.

❖To assemble box, wrap box side around inside bottom cardboard. Hold in place and mark overlap. Hot-glue one short edge of box side to opposite edge at overlap mark. Working upside down, slip inside bottom into box side $\frac{1}{16}$" down from edge. Hot-glue in place.

❖For ribbon hinge, hot-glue $\frac{1}{2}$" piece of $\frac{5}{8}$"-wide satin ribbon to top, inside edge of box side at left edge of over-lapping cardboard. Cut a $1\frac{7}{8}$" circle from quilt batting. Hot-glue batting to inside bottom of box.

❖With right side up, finger-gather inside box bottom lining fabric onto lining strip while hot-gluing in place. (An alternative is to gather-stitch around outer edge of lining fabric $\frac{1}{4}$" from edge. Adjust gathers to fit strip and hot-glue in place.)

❖When all fabric has been hot-glued to strip, strip becomes circular and inside out. Flip lining strip so fabric is right side out. Turn down cardboard strip so lining has finished edge. Hot-glue wrong side of strip to inside of box side at top edge, keeping ribbon hinge extended out from box.

❖Begin hot-gluing at center of strip. Where cardboard edges meet, adjust lining strip, larger or smaller, as needed, depending on fabric weight.

❖With right side down, rest inside lid into top edge of box and hold in place. Hot-glue ribbon hinge onto wrong side of inside lid, creating a snug fit so lid will open. Center and hot-glue wrong side of inside lid to right side of middle lid.

•Using Ribbons

❖Refer to General Instructions on pages 19-25.

❖Take apart small velvet cabbage (or other 9-petal velvet item) so there are nine petals. Hot-glue petals to underside of box, cupping petals upward onto box side.

❖Make two Gathered Leaves by cutting 1"-wide hunter green ribbon into two 4" lengths. Hot-glue gathered edge of leaves to underside of box. Hot-glue wrong side of base to underside of box.

❖Using industrial-strength glue and toothpick, attach two antique brass mirror charms together.

❖Flute velvet wine ribbon around entire underside edge of pincushion top.

❖Fold $\frac{1}{2}$"-wide lace in half, matching short ends. Seam lace. Gather-stitch along bottom edge of lace. Tightly gather and secure thread. Slip bottom edge of antique brass mirror charms through center of lace ruffle. Set aside.

❖Thread heavyweight needle with four strands of thread, knotted at end. Stitch needle up through cardboard underside of pincushion top. Stitch needle through rings of antique brass mirror charms, then take needle back down through cardboard. Bring needle up again through center of pincushion top, stitch through ring on antique brass mirror charms, then down again through cardboard. Pull thread tight so pincushion top begins to be tufted. Repeat above process until tufting feels secure. It is not necessary to stitch through ring on antique brass mirror charms again. Secure thread on underside of pincushion top. Slide lace ruffle down antique brass mirrors to meet pincushion top. Invisibly hot-glue lace to center of pincushion top, enabling antique brass mirror charms to stand straight up.

❖Make small bow from 9" of 4mm olive green ribbon. Hot-glue knot of small bow to inside of box at top edge where cardboards overlap.

❖Layer three shades of remaining 4mm ribbons. Make into small bow. Hot-glue knot of bow underneath lace ruffle on left side. Knot each ribbon end.

•Finishing

❖Using industrial-strength glue, attach two beads each to corsage pins. Let glue dry thoroughly. Place in pincushion top.

Pincushion Box Patterns
Enlarge 240%

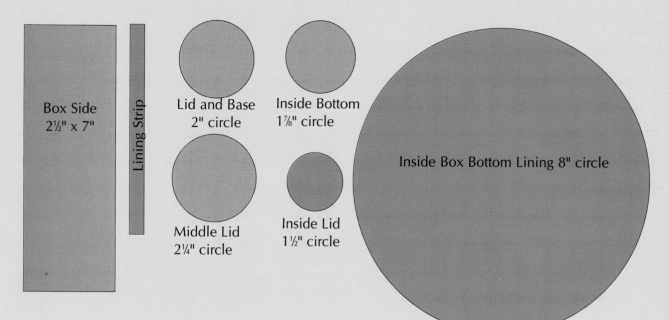

Box Side
2½" x 7"

Lining Strip

Lid and Base
2" circle

Inside Bottom
1⅞" circle

Inside Box Bottom Lining 8" circle

Middle Lid
2¼" circle

Inside Lid
1½" circle

Wool Pillow

Shown on page 115.

Materials

Fabric: wool, off-white, 9" x 15"

Thread: coordinating

Silk ribbons: 4mm — two shades of green, 1 yd. each

Embroidery wool floss: green, mauve, burgundy, blue, green, gold, rose, dk. rose, lt. rose

Tassels: ivory, small (4)

Stuffing: polyester

Tools

Needles: chenille (size 20); milliner's (sizes 3-9)

Scissors: fabric

Sewing machine

Directions

•Making Patterns and Cutting Fabrics

❖Using fabric scissors, cut one 9" x 7½" piece from wool fabric.

•Embroidering

❖Refer to General Instructions on pages 14-19.

❖Refer to Transfer Sheet and Placement Diagram on page 119. Embroider design following Ribbon Embroidery Color and Stitch Guide on page 119.

•Finishing

❖Cut embroidered wool to 7½" square. Cut a second 7½" square of wool. Taper pillow corners to eliminate bulk. Using coordinating thread, with right sides together, stitch front to back, leaving 3" opening on one side. Turn right side out. Using polyester stuffing, stuff pillow. Stitch opening closed. Stitch tassels to corners.

Wool Pillow • Ribbon Embroidery Color and Stitch Guide
Silk ribbons listed below are 4mm unless otherwise indicated.
Embroidery floss listed below is three strands unless otherwise indicated.

Step		Ribbon and Floss Color	Stitch
1	Rose	Dk. and Lt. Rose Floss, Mauve Floss	Wool Rose Stitch, Stem Stitch
	✿Stitch center of wool rose dk. rose and middle lt. rose. Highlight outer edge using Stem Stitch with mauve floss.		
2	Flower	Dk. Rose Floss, Mauve Floss	Bullion Stitch, Stem Stitch
	✿Stitch 10 wrap Bullion Stitches for center of two flowers. Highlight outer edge using Stem Stitch with mauve floss.		
3	Stem	Green Floss	Stem Stitch
4	Flower	Dk. Rose Floss, Burgundy Floss, Mauve Floss	Straight Stitch, Fly Stitch
	✿Stitch 5-petal flower with dk. rose floss. Highlight center of flowers with burgundy floss. Highlight tips of each petal using Fly Stitch with mauve floss.		
5	Rosebud	Lt. Rose Floss, Green Floss	Straight Stitch
	✿Straight-stitch four flower buds with lt. rose floss. Highlight each bud with green floss.		
6	Leaves	Green Floss	Feather Stitch
7	Forget-Me-Nots	Blue Floss, Gold Floss	Colonial Knot
	✿Stitch forget-me-nots with blue floss. Stitch center with gold floss.		
8	Leaves	Two Shades Green Ribbon	Ribbon Stitch, Cross-over Lazy Daisy with Elongated Tip
9	Leaves	Green Floss	Fly Stitch
	✿Scatter Fly Stitch for leaf texture.		

✿*Additional Stitch Information*

Wool Pillow Transfer Sheet
Enlarge 155%

Wool Pillow Placement Diagram

Powder Puff

Shown on page 115.
Materials

Thread: coordinating

Assorted ribbons: ⅝"-wide satin, olive green,
½ yd.; 1½"-wide bias, delicate shade,
1½ yds.

Lace: 1"-wide, two styles, ⅜ yd. each

Doily: 6" filet

Powder puff: 3"-diameter, white

Dowel: wooden, 6" long, ¼"-wide

Tools

Glue: hot glue gun and glue sticks

Iron and ironing board

Needles: hand-sewing

Scissors: fabric

Directions

•Assembling

❖Refer to General Instructions on pages 8-11.

❖Diagonally wrap dowel with ⅝"-wide satin olive green ribbon. Open powder puff at seam ½". Insert unfinished end of wrapped dowel into opening so 1" of dowel is within powder puff. Stitch or hot-glue dowel in place. Stitch or hot-glue opening closed.

❖Gather-stitch around doily center so stitches are equally spaced from center with a 1½"-diameter circle. Tightly gather and secure thread. Stitch or hot-glue gathered doily center to powder puff top. Stitch doily to powder puff edges.

❖Gather-stitch edge of one piece of 1"-wide lace, tapering stitches at both ends. Pull stitches so lace measures 3". Stitch or hot-glue gathered edge of lace to powder puff top over doily so finished edge of lace covers outer edge of powder puff. Repeat with second piece of 1"-wide lace.

•Using Ribbons

❖Refer to General Instructions on page 21.

❖Fray edge along entire length of bias cut ribbon ¼" deep. Repeat for opposite edge.

❖Fold one long edge of ribbon up ⅝" and press along fold to hold in place. Do not allow iron to touch frayed edges.

❖Stitch entire length of frayed ribbon into a Gathered Rosebud.

•Finishing

❖Hot-glue Gathered Rosebud to center top of powder puff.

Oval Box

Shown on page 115.
Materials

Fabrics: velvet: olive green, 7" x 15"

Thread: coordinating

Silk ribbons: 4mm — rose/green ombre,
dk. rose, deep rose, ¾ yd. each

Hand-dyed ribbon: 4mm — gold, 1½ yds.
Assorted ribbons: ¾"-wide satin, dk. green,
¼ yd.; 1½"-wide velvet, mauve/gold, ¼ yd.;
¼"-wide brown, 1¼ yds.

Seed beads: #10 — olive green (23)

Beads: garnet-shaded, large and medium
(1 each)

Bugle beads: mauve (5)

Pearls: ecru, small (9), medium (5)

Charms: antique brass flowers (2); antique
brass corner piece (1)

Cardboard: heavy, 4" x 8"; lightweight,
2" x 9"

Quilt batting: 3" x 3"

Continued on page 121

Continued from page 120

Wire: 22-gauge, 12"

Tools

Glue: craft, thin-bodied; hot glue gun and glue sticks; industrial-strength

Old paintbrush or 3" paint roller

Marking tool

Needles: chenille (size 20); hand-sewing

Scissors: craft; fabric

Wire cutters

Directions

•Making Patterns and Cutting Fabrics

❖Refer to General Instructions on pages 8-11.

❖Refer to Oval Box Patterns on page 122.

❖Using craft scissors, cut one box side, one lid side, and one box top from lightweight cardboard. Cut one inside bottom, one base, and one lid from heavy cardboard.

❖Using fabric scissors, cut one 2½" x 8½" from velvet fabric for box side. Cut one 2¾" x 9" from velvet fabric for lid side. Cut one box top from quilt batting.

❖Add ¾" seam allowance. Cut one inside bottom, one base, and one lid from velvet fabric.

❖Place and label fabric cuts with corresponding cardboard pieces.

•Assembling

❖Refer to General Instructions on pages 11-13 and 15.

❖Using thin-bodied craft glue and old paintbrush or 3" paint roller, laminate base, inside bottom, and lid with velvet fabric.

❖Place box side fabric on work surface, wrong side up. Laminate box side cardboard onto box side fabric, ¼" from one long edge and centered

between short edges. Trim excess fabric from bottom edge of cardboard. Place box side onto work surface, uncovered side up. Glue ½" of one short edge of fabric. Wrap short edge over itself at cardboard's edge. Do not glue or cut remaining short edge of fabric.

❖With uncovered side up, roll box side using round hot glue stick, or anything similar in diameter. Join and glue short edges of box side by overlapping finished short edge to tab edge and butting cardboard edges to each other.

❖Repeat previous three assembling steps with box lid strip.

❖Working upside down, slip inside bottom into box side, ¹⁄₁₆" down from trimmed edge of box side. Using hot glue gun and glue stick, hot-glue in place. Hold until dry. Snugly extend fabric down over uncovered side of box side. Hot-glue raw edge of extended fabric to wrong side of inside bottom. Slip lid into box lid strip. Repeat for box side.

❖With wrong side up, place box bottom on work surface. Flute while hot-gluing ¼"-wide brown velvet ribbon to underside of box bottom, extending ribbon ⅛" past box edge. With wrong sides together, hot-glue base to box bottom.

❖Wrap and hot-glue 1½"-wide velvet ribbon around box lid strip, overlapping ribbon at one long side. Finger-gather and glue ribbon over onto lid.

•Embroidery

❖Refer to General Instructions on pages 14-19.

❖Cut 4" square velvet fabric. Trace box top cardboard pattern onto wrong side of velvet fabric. Baste-stitch on traced line. Embroider design onto 4" square velvet fabric inside baste stitch following Ribbon Embroidery Color and Stitch Guide on page 122.

•Finishing

❖Refer to General Instructions on pages 11-15.

❖Pad cardboard box top with quilt batting. Trim flush to cardboard's edge and bevel inward slightly. Trim embroidered fabric ½" outside baste stitch. Using craft glue, wrap and glue cardboard with embroidered fabric. Clip curves, trim corners, and points as needed.

❖Stitch antique brass flowers to bottom edge of embroidery using coordinating thread. Using industrial-strength glue, attach antique brass corner piece to top right edge.

❖Using hot glue gun and glue stick, flute while hot-gluing ¼"-wide velvet brown ribbon to underside of box top, on three sides only. Cut ¾"-wide satin dk. green ribbon in half lengthwise. Gather-stitch along one long edge of one piece of ribbon, creating a fan shape. Tightly gather and secure thread. Repeat with second piece of ribbon. Hot-glue gathered edge to underside edge of box top at right side and center left side.

❖For beaded sprays, slip a pearl through 6" length of 22-gauge wire. Fold wire in half so pearl is at top of fold. Slip both wires through the following beads: bugle-pearl-garnet-pearl-bugle-seed-bugle. Twist wire ends together. For second spray, slip a pearl through another 6" length of 22-gauge wire. Fold wire in half so pearl is at top of fold. Slip both wires through the following beads: pearl-pearl-garnet-pearl-bugle-seed-bugle. Twist wire ends together. Hot-glue sprays to underside of box top, at bottom right edge.

❖Hot-glue box top to lid.

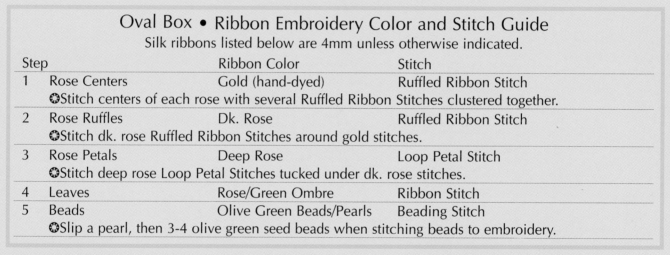

Oval Box • Ribbon Embroidery Color and Stitch Guide
Silk ribbons listed below are 4mm unless otherwise indicated.

Step		Ribbon Color	Stitch
1	Rose Centers	Gold (hand-dyed)	Ruffled Ribbon Stitch
	✲Stitch centers of each rose with several Ruffled Ribbon Stitches clustered together.		
2	Rose Ruffles	Dk. Rose	Ruffled Ribbon Stitch
	✲Stitch dk. rose Ruffled Ribbon Stitches around gold stitches.		
3	Rose Petals	Deep Rose	Loop Petal Stitch
	✲Stitch deep rose Loop Petal Stitches tucked under dk. rose stitches.		
4	Leaves	Rose/Green Ombre	Ribbon Stitch
5	Beads	Olive Green Beads/Pearls	Beading Stitch
	✲Slip a pearl, then 3-4 olive green seed beads when stitching beads to embroidery.		

✲Additional Stitch Information

Oval Box Patterns Enlarge 240%

Inside Bottom

Lid

Base

Box Top

Box Side

Lid Side

Oval Box Placement Diagram

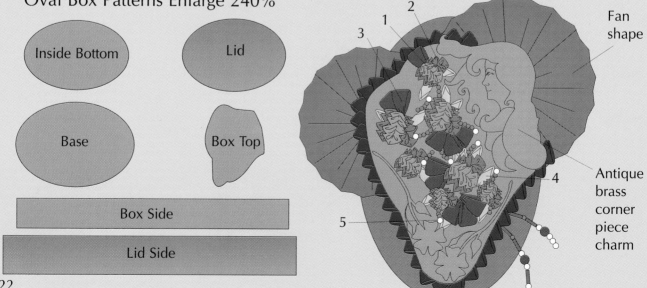

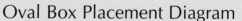

Fan shape

Antique brass corner piece charm

Lingerie Bag

Lingerie Bag

Shown on page 123.

Materials

Fabrics: moiré, ecru, 12½" x 7½", for envelope flap; moiré, ecru, 12½" x 7½", for flap lining; moiré, ecru, 12½" x 11½", for back piece; moiré, ecru, 20" x 12½", for lining piece; organdy or voile fabric, 12½" x 11½"; scraps, 5" x 4", ecru (5); ivory (5); tan (5); peach (5)

Thread: coordinating

Silk ribbons: 4mm — lt. avocado, banana, cream, lt. dusty rose, gray purple, jungle green, lavender, pale grass, lt. periwinkle, salmon, 3 yds. each; 7mm — lt. coral, cream, 3 yds. each

Lace: ⅝"-wide, ¾ yd.; assorted narrow lace trims, ½ yd. (5); small lace appliqués (6)

Embroidery floss: lt. olive green, med. olive green, lt. tan

Double-sided fusible web: ½ yd.

Fusible interfacing: 6" x 8"

Tools

Iron and ironing board

Needles: chenille (size 20); embroidery

Scissors: fabric

Sewing machine

Directions

•Making Patterns and Cutting Fabrics

❖Refer to General Instructions on pages 8-11.

❖Using fabric scissors, cut moiré, and organdy fabrics.

❖Refer to Front of Bag Placement Diagram on page 125. Fuse scraps of fabric onto double-sided

fusible web, following manufacturer's instructions. Cut out random shapes.

•Assembling

❖Arrange and fuse fabric shapes on 12½" x 11½" organdy for front of bag.

❖With coordinating threads, machine-stitch narrow zigzag around each fused fabric shape and at outer edges.

❖Machine-stitch assorted lace trims along all seams. Randomly sew on lace appliqués. *Optional: Weave ribbon through some of the lace trims.*

•Embroidery

❖Refer to General Instructions on pages 14-19.

❖Refer to Lingerie Bag Flap Transfer Sheet and Flap Stitching Placement Diagram on page 126. Embroider design onto envelope flap fabric following Ribbon Embroidery Color and Stitch Guide on page 125.

•Finishing

❖Refer to Envelope Flap Diagram on page 125. Shape bottom edge of embroidered flap and flap lining in shape of an envelope flap. With right sides together, machine-stitch flap lining to embroidered flap with ½" seam, leaving top edge unstitched. Trim seam and bulk from inside corners. Turn right side out. Press. Machine-topstitch lace to edges of embroidered flap.

❖With right sides together, machine-stitch embroidered flap to back piece. Press seam down. Machine-stitch front of bag to back piece at bottom and sides with ½" seams.

❖With right sides together, fold lining piece in half to measure 12½" x 10". Machine-stitch ½" seams at sides, leaving 5" opening on one of side seams.

❖With right sides together, slip lining over bag. Have embroidered flap hidden inward. Machine-stitch at top edge with ½" seam. Turn bag right side out through side opening of lining. Machine-topstitch top edge of lingerie bag, keeping embroidered flap free. Stitch opening of lining closed.

Lingerie Bag • Ribbon Embroidery Color and Stitch Guide

Silk ribbons listed below are 4mm unless otherwise indicated.
Embroidery floss listed below is three strands unless otherwise indicated.

Step		Ribbon and Floss Color	Stitch
1	Peony Center, buds	Salmon	Bullion Lazy Daisy, Straight Stitch
2	Peony Bottom Layer	Lt. Dusty Rose	Ribbon Stitch, 1-Twist Ribbon Stitch
3	Peony Ruffles	Banana	Pistil Stitch
4	Large Peony Petals	Cream, 7mm	Ribbon Stitch, 1-Twist Ribbon Stitch
5	Stems, Peony	Med. Olive Green Floss	Couching Stitch
6	Stems, Gladiola	Med. Olive Green Floss	Couching Stitch (6 strands)
7	Stems, Freesia	Lt. Olive Green Floss	Couching Stitch (6 strands)
8	Freesia	Cream	Lazy Daisy, Ribbon Stitch
9	Leaves	Pale Grass	Bullion Lazy Daisy
10	Leaves	Jungle Green	Ribbon Stitch, Lazy Daisy
11	Gladiola, Large Petals	Lt. Coral, 7mm	Loop Petal Stitch, Lazy Daisy
12	Gladiola, Small Petals	Salmon	Loop Petal Stitch
13	Stamens	Lt. Tan Floss	Pistil Stitch
14	Lilacs	Gray Purple	French Knot
15	Lilacs	Lt. Periwinkle	French Knot
16	Lilacs	Lavender	French Knot
17	Leaves	Lt. Avocado	Ribbon Stitch

Front of Bag Placement Diagram

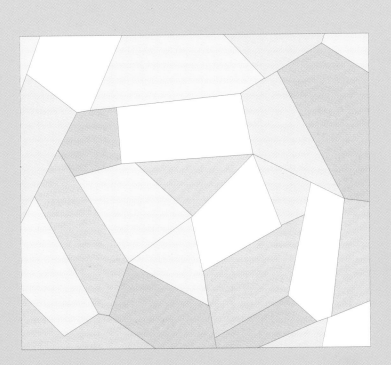

Envelope Flap Diagram

125

Lingerie Bag Flap Transfer Sheet
Enlarge 120%

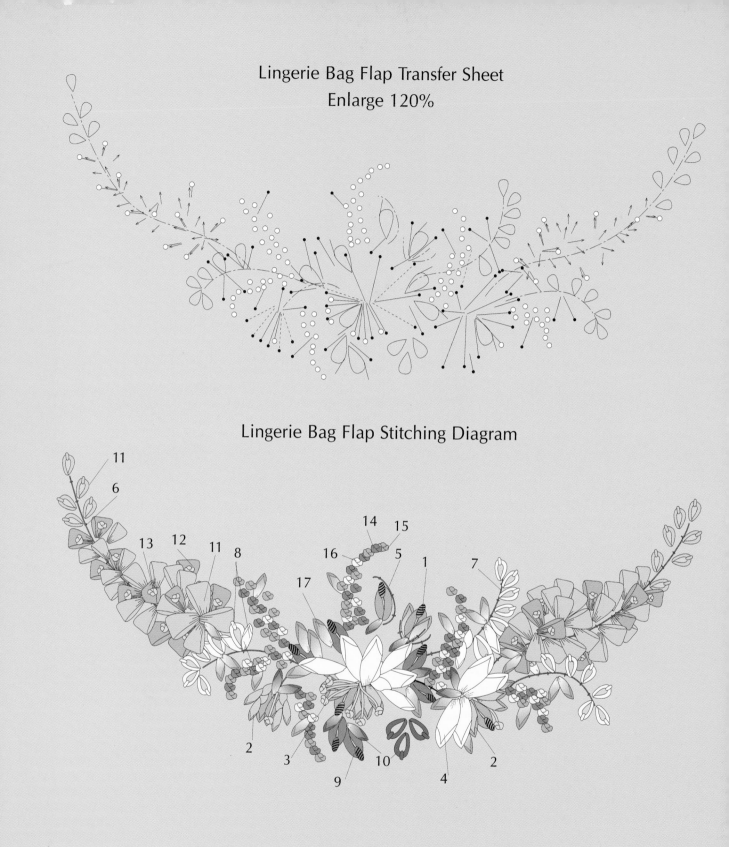

Lingerie Bag Flap Stitching Diagram

Index

Index

Metric Conversions

mm-millimetres   cm-centimetres
inches to millimetres and centimetres

inches	mm	cm	inches	cm	inches	cm
⅛	3	0.3	9	22.9	30	76.2
¼	6	0.6	10	25.4	31	78.7
½	13	1.3	12	30.5	33	83.8
⅝	16	1.6	13	33.0	34	86.4
¾	19	1.9	14	35.6	35	88.9
⅞	22	2.2	15	38.1	36	91.4
1	25	2.5	16	40.6	37	94.0
1¼	32	3.2	17	43.2	38	96.5
1½	38	3.8	18	45.7	39	99.1
1¾	44	4.4	19	48.3	40	101.6
2	51	5.1	20	50.8	41	104.1
2½	64	6.4	21	53.3	42	106.7
3	76	7.6	22	55.9	43	109.2
3½	89	8.9	23	58.4	44	111.8
4	102	10.2	24	61.0	45	114.3
4½	114	11.4	25	63.5	46	116.8
5	127	12.7	26	66.0	47	119.4
6	152	15.2	27	68.6	48	121.9
7	178	17.8	28	71.1	49	124.5
8	203	20.3	29	73.7	50	127.0